Walking
A How-To Guide for the Novice Camino de Santiago Pilgrim
2017 Edition

A way marker on the Camino de Santiago

If life came with such clear-cut instructions, we wouldn't need to undertake pilgrimage, and what a pity that would be.

Acknowledgements

I want to thank all of the many people I met on the Camino, and who enriched the experience for me: the American ex-pat working in London, the four Scandinavian septuagenarians, my Aussie friend, my Kiwi friend, my Boston friend. What a wonderful cast of characters. I wish you all a buen Camino.

Thank you, Marty and Kevin, for always being there for me. Thank you, family, for listening to me talk endlessly about the Camino for so many months before and after my trip. Thank you, parents, for sending me to good schools. Thank you, teachers, who taught me how to write. Thank you, Jim, who, though you don't know it, finally made me see the true value of faith.

Thank you, Rick Steves, for your excellent television and guidebook series, which make traveling to Europe so easy and enjoyable.

And thank you, readers, for giving this book a chance.

To Readers and Pilgrims

The challenge in writing a travel and how-to book is that the information you need is constantly changing, and there's a lot of it to know. I've done my best to make sure that the information contained here is accurate and that it is up-to-date as of publication.

Table of Contents

Part I

The Camino de Santiago

1. Introduction

The routine of backpacking is simple. Every day is pretty much like the day that came before it: you wake up, you walk, you eat breakfast, you walk, you eat lunch, you walk, you eat dinner, you sleep, you wake up, and you walk again. The venue determines whether you get to shower at the end of the day or wash clothes, whether you have to pitch a tent, whether you're cooking over a fire or dining at a trailside café, but the essential activities of backpacking are always the same. Whether you're doing it for six months or a week, it doesn't change. That's the basis for this book. Whether you're walking the entire Camino or just a section, all pilgrims have the same needs.

The idea for this book came to me one day as I was walking a section of the Katy Trail in St. Charles, Missouri. The Katy Trail used to be a rail bed and is made of crushed, white stone, so on that July day, even though it was fairly early, the heat radiating from the path had me turning around after a short 3.5 miles. I was carrying about 50 pounds and sucking down plenty of water, but the heat and humidity were winning as the sun got higher. As I walked, to keep my mind off of the heat I considered everything I had learned about backpacking over the last several years as it became my favorite hobby.

If you're like me, since deciding to do the Camino, you've started reading just about everything there is about the Camino and long-distance backpacking, and you've re-read much of it. As I read, and especially as I re-read, I was perturbed by the lack of detail in some books claiming to be the definitive how-to on the Camino. "Take a lightweight backpack." Gee, what inspired advice!

In other cases, the advice is downright bad, if not dangerous. "Use a needle to puncture a blister." Wow, food for thought as a doctor is telling you in Spanish that your foot is infected and you need to go home.

What needs to be added to the literature of the Camino is advice from a backpacker. Detailed advice, like how to pick out a backpack *and* how to use the thing; why you should use trekking poles; what it's like to stay in an albergue; and how to properly treat a blister.

I'm no expert on the entire Camino. Neither am I an expert backpacker in the vein of those who have walked the entire Appalachian Trail or the Pacific Crest Trail. I can't offer you detailed information on all the villages you'll pass through or the elevation gain and loss, and I can't regale you with advice learned while traversing thousands of miles on America's longest trails.

Instead I offer you my advice as a Camino veteran and as someone who spends many a weekend out on the trail somewhere. I regularly take day hikes and do short overnights, carrying just The Ten Essentials or several days' worth of supplies. In learning to hike and in making my pilgrimage to Santiago, I made mistakes, I sought advice from others, I read every Camino guide and narrative and how-to I could find, and I learned. That's what this book is: detailed backpacking advice learned the hard way and applied to the Camino de Santiago.

This book is from the perspective of someone who walked the most common Camino route – the Camino Frances – but almost all of the advice can apply to any route, and much of it applies to pilgrims attempting the Camino by bicycle. It is by no means the definitive book on the subject, I am no means an expert, and I encourage you to read all you can about the journey before you go so that you can make the best-informed choices for yourself.

With my experience and mistakes in mind, I offer you this guide to the Camino that I hope will prove useful to you, and especially to novice hikers taking on this great and meaningful undertaking.

2. A brief history of the Camino de Santiago

The Camino de Santiago – The Way of Saint James – is a network of pilgrimage routes converging on Santiago de Compostela in northwestern Spain at the foot of the cathedral built over the bones of the Saint. For over a thousand years, paupers, popes, and kings have walked the Camino seeking the blessings of Saint James and as penance for their sins.

Long before the Camino was ever associated with Saint James, pagans walked the route not to Santiago but three days further, to Finisterre, The End of the Land. It was at the time believed to be the end of the world, the westernmost land in Europe (though Cabo de Roca in Portugal is actually westernmost mainland Europe). No one knows why they undertook this journey. One theory popular with new age types is that the Camino is a "Ley Line," a channel where the energy of stars is reflected back by the earth. A second theory is that as the westernmost point of land in Europe, the pagan pilgrims believed the souls of the dead went to Finisterre before making their final journey across the ocean; this theory has little documentary evidence to back it up, but then the Celtic pagans of Galicia weren't much for record keeping. A third theory is that it had something to do with following the stars to the ocean – the most common route does sort of line up with the Milky Way.

In any case, it doesn't really matter if or why people walked the Camino before Christianity came to Iberia. After so many centuries, the exact details of what came before the Camino are shrouded in myth and time. The same is true of the origins of the pilgrimage, but here is the story as best it can be cobbled together.

Around 813, a hermit named Pelayo followed unusually bright stars to a field where he found a decapitated skeleton. Pelayo contacted the local authorities, and Bishop Theodomar declared the skeleton to be that of Saint James the Greater, whose name in Spanish is rendered as Santiago, one of the twelve Apostles of Christ.

Following Christ's instructions to go forward and spread his Gospel, Saint James is said to have sailed to the Iberian Peninsula, where he met only a little success preaching to the pagan Iberians. He returned to Jerusalem where he ran afoul of the Roman authorities for his aggressive proselytizing and was beheaded by Herod Agrippa in 42 A.D, giving him the dubious honor of being the first apostle martyred. According to legend, James's friends recovered his body and placed it on a stone boat (no sails, no oars, no rudder) which was divinely transported back to Spain where the few Iberians he converted buried his body inland in Galicia.

At the time Pelayo discovered the body, most of the Iberian Peninsula was under the control of the Muslim Moors, but northwestern Spain, the region known as Galicia, was still under Christian control. As Christians attempted to reclaim Spain from the Moors (a seven-centuries-long struggle known as the *Reconquista*), it was politically convenient for the Church and kings of Christian Spain to have a figure to rally around. Saint James fit their needs: the Christian population of northern Spain grew as towns and cities formed along the route pilgrims walked to pay homage to the relics of Saint James, and military aid to fight the Moors came in from Christian kings and princes further east. Of the many miracles attributed to Saint James, the one that earned him his cognomen is appearing on horseback at the Battle of Clavijo in 844 and killing 60,000 Moors. Hence, Santiago Matamoros – Saint James the Moor Slayer. In actuality, the legend was established centuries after the battle, which never happened. The *Reconquista* was completed in 1492 (just in time for the victorious Catholic monarchs, Ferdinand and Isabella, to fund a Genoese sailor looking for a new route to India).

Modern scholars of course doubt that the body Pelayo found belongs to Saint James, but they do agree that the reliquary in the cathedral contains a decapitated skeleton. One theory is that the body is that of Priscillian, the first Christian executed by other Christians for heresy in 385 in Trier in modern Germany. No community would accept the body for burial, so it was transported back to Galicia, where he had been Bishop of Ávila, and buried in an empty field. Or so the theory goes.

A church was built over Saint James' grave, and a cathedral was eventually built beginning in 1075 and completed in 1211, with the current Baroque façade completed in 1740. Since the 9th century, Christians have made the journey to Santiago on foot. Medieval pilgrims started at their front doors, often carrying nothing but a walking stick and a gourd for drinking. These pilgrims faced a lack of food, harsh weather, and bandits; they relied on the strangers whose homes they passed for food and shelter. The Catholic order of the Knights Templar, and then the Hospitallers of Saint John after the Templars were destroyed, were charged with protecting pilgrims on the Way. The arduousness of the journey is evident: modern pilgrims pass by numerous pilgrims' cemeteries along the Way. For most medieval people, such a pilgrimage was their only chance to travel more than a few miles from where they were born.

The Middle Ages in Europe have been called the Age of Faith, with approximately one church for every 40 or 50 people. A larger proportion of medieval Europe made the pilgrimage then than today, with many pilgrims carrying stone or lime from quarries along the Camino to build churches in towns further on. The popularity of the pilgrimage is best demonstrated by the pillar at the center of the Portico da Gloria, the entryway at the front of the Cathedral. In the center of this intricately carved tympanum is a pillar depicting Saint James and the Tree of Jesse. About chest high on the pillar, the stone has been worn smooth with five indentations about an inch deep radiating out from the center – the imprint of the millions of pilgrim hands placed in that spot since the pillar was completed in 1188.

The Camino was mostly forgotten in the tumult of the Black Death, the Reformation and the dynastic wars of the 17th, 18th and 19th centuries, only to be rediscovered at the beginning of the 21st. The most popular route is the Camino Frances, which begins in Saint Jean Pied de Port on the French side of the Pyrenees and continues about 800km (500 miles) to Santiago, about a month-long walk. While just a handful of pilgrims completed the journey thirty years ago, over 200,000 completed the journey in 2014.

Modern pilgrims undertake the journey for a variety of reasons, some religious and spiritual but mostly for the adventure, health, or to meditate on the future course of their lives. You don't have to be Catholic to walk the Camino – it's a journey for everyone.

A pilgrim is said to have completed the Camino if he walks (or rides a horse or donkey) the final 100km to Santiago, or bikes the last 200km. The pilgrim carries a *credencial*, a pilgrim's passport, that is stamped at *albergues*, churches, monasteries, cafes, and even police stations along the way to prove she has walked that distance. Presenting the *credencial* to the cathedral authorities, the pilgrim is given the *compostela*, a certificate attesting to the fact that he has completed the journey. In holy years and on certain dates, a pilgrim completing the journey and obtaining the *compostela* is granted a plenary indulgence if he makes his confession, attends Mass, prays for the intentions of the Holy Father, and undertakes some charitable work.

Whereas the modern pilgrim then proceeds home by train or airplane, medieval pilgrims turned around and walked back home. They would wear the scallop shell, a symbol of the pilgrimage, for the rest of their lives to show all they had completed the journey.

3. Why I walk the Camino

I'm probably the last person most would expect to be an avid backpacker. I'm essentially a statistician by trade and a bit of a homebody (cue friends and family laughing). That I spend my weekends in quick-dry shorts with a sweatband around my forehead surprises people. Sure, I come from a family that camped when we were kids, and we'd go fly fishing pretty regularly, but none of us hiked. It was a hobby I toyed with when I moved to Pennsylvania for graduate school, but after I moved to DC for work and got rid of my car, I gave up all my outdoor activities.

Neither was I an athlete. Sure, I wanted to be, but I lost that genetic lottery. If I round up, I'm five-foot-six. On top of that, I've loved food for as long as I can remember, and for as long as I can remember, I've been overweight. At my heaviest, I was 273 pounds. I've yo-yoed my weight twice now, and each time I ended up caving after about 30 pounds of weight loss and put it all back on and then some. My interest in hiking was revived during one of those periods when I was doing well watching my weight.

One year, and none of my Christmas gifts fit me. That was a pretty good wake up call. I put myself on a simple but strict diet and worked out 8 times a week. I hate the gym. It's boring; the only way to make it interesting is to observe the weirdness of the people around you (like the exhibitionist couple that chose the gym as a place to make out in public – you know who you are, and you're not fooling anybody).

At some point during that period, I either saw the *Rick Steves' Europe* episode about the Camino or the Martin Sheen movie *The Way*, and it looked like a lot of fun. At the time, I was planning my first vacation since those childhood family trips, and it suddenly occurred to me that I could do the Camino. I had never been to Europe, I didn't speak Spanish, but I decided to go. I read all about it. I read Camino memoirs, I read guidebooks, I read packing lists, I read forums, I read about hiking other trails, and I made the arrangements.

I started hiking to prepare for the Camino, and it quickly turned into a passion. For me, hiking is like Zen. A Zen Buddhist monk I once knew called it "doing not-doing." When a professional basketball player is making a layup, you know they stopped thinking about *how* to make a layup years ago – they just do it. The better you are at hiking, the more you do it without thinking about it and just absorb the experience.

Hiking is a singular activity. When you're hiking, you're only doing the one thing (I'm a millennial – hiking is the only time when I'm ever doing only one thing). When I'm on the trail, I can disconnect. In an age where you're expected to be reachable by email and cellphone all the time, the trail is where I'm unreachable. I can't get enough of that feeling. A lot of people say that on a long-distance hike is the freest they ever feel. Even on a day hike, for a few short hours of a random Sunday, the only thing that matters is me taking myself up over the next hill and down the other side, and it matters because I decided that it matters. Tomorrow other things will matter again, but right now, it's just my backpack, the trail, and me. For me, hiking is a mental release as much as a physical one.

Besides that, just because I didn't have the talent to be an athlete in terms of organized sports didn't mean I didn't want to be. I played sports in high school, but I was bad at them. Physical accomplishment was out of reach for me. I could earn two masters degrees and land a great job and win some recognition for it, but I couldn't win a basketball game or throw a football with a decent spiral. It dawned on me, though, that there were athletic things I could do that most other people didn't. To wit, I could sling 50 pounds on my back and walk 18 miles and endure umpteen kinds of pain and enjoy it. Instead of being daunting, the distance and the pain became the accomplishment. Proving to myself that I could do it was addicting. In retrospect, the worst hikes are my favorite stories to tell:

- July 4th and 5th on the C&O Canal Towpath on the banks of the Potomac River. I set my sights on a campsite 26 miles up the trail and ended up going 18 miles before turning around and heading back two miles to the last site. I'm not sure why my feet hurt so badly that day, but they did. I was practically in shock when I sat down at a picnic table and took my boots off. Some fellow campers invited me over to their fire for the evening, and a third gentleman joined us. The former were Air Force reservists who worked for a defense contractor in Maryland. The latter was a retired doctor and a long-distance hiker. He had done the Appalachian Trail, the Camino, and was doing the entire C&O (180 miles). I tried cowboy camping that night, but the bugs were unbearable, so I got up at 1am and hobbled back the 16 miles to the trailhead. It took me 12 hours, stopping every mile to rest my throbbing feet, and I committed a Tex-Mex takeout atrocity that evening.

- The following May I set out to do the first 13 miles of the Ozark Trail going southbound. I ended up stopping after a hard eight miles and shared a cliff-side campsite with a young Army officer from Fort Leonard Wood and his girlfriend. He proposed to her right there. I think of sharing their special evening with them more than the fact that I ran out of water on the next day's very hot morning with about two uphill miles to go. And I got stung by a bee.

- A couple of days before my 28th birthday, I went hiking at Bennett Spring State Park while my dad fished downstream. A park ranger spotted me with my pack and asked if I had bug repellant; I didn't. I walked to a natural tunnel that wasn't worth seeing and then hiked back. The hike was taking much longer than anticipated, in large part because I was stopping so frequently to pick ticks, *dozens of them*, off my legs before they could find a spot to dig in. I also found out that the park's signs are wrong and the trail is 1.5 miles longer than they say.

You know what day I remember most from my Camino? The longest day. It had been unseasonably hot, and that day, the day before I was to arrive in Santiago de Compostela, was perfectly sunny and not hot at all. I met another American a few days before and we hiked together on and off and shared accommodations. We arrived at what the guidebook said was the best place to spend the night, but we were both feeling good, and the next village was just 3km further on. It turned out to be a rough three kilometers, and my feet were hurting, so when we found out the albergue was full, we were disappointed and walked on another 6km or so. We walked a total of 34km that day (21 miles), a longer day than most on the Camino. The lousy hotel and lousy dinner that night were heaven-sent.

The Camino for me, however, is so much more than a physical challenge. It's spiritual, it's emotional, and above all, it's human. I was raised Catholic (Catholic mother, Jewish father), and I've struggled with faith my entire life.

For many years, I considered myself an atheist, and let's face up to facts: in society in general but especially in America, there really is no viler a pariah than an atheist. I was never what some would call an evangelical atheist; I didn't care what religion others believed or didn't, and I still don't. I attended a Jesuit high school, though, and I took four years of theology as required, and being a contrary individual anyway, plus being a teenager, I was apt to debate my theology teachers just for the sake of debate. But nonetheless I listened, and much of what they said stayed with me, and I kept thinking about it, and to this day I consider some of their lessons the most valuable I ever learned.

When I got to college, I made only one good friend, an evangelical Southern Baptist. I was amazed at his faith. He believed that God would take care of him if he gave himself up to God. In other words, if he trusted God, he need not worry. God to him was a parent always half a step behind you in case you stumble. I was jealous of that kind of faith. I didn't have faith, and I had a hard time imagining how I might develop that kind of faith – I didn't believe in God, I didn't feel any connection to the Catholic Church, and I didn't see what it could do for me.

Several months before deciding to walk the Camino, I decided to read up on the history of the Catholic Church. You know what the Catholic Church is? It's the last living vestige of the Roman Empire. Once Christianity became the state religion of the Roman Empire, the Church was transformed almost overnight, and once the Empire fell, the structure of the Empire was preserved in the Church: the Pope is analogous to the Emperor, and for centuries, the kings of Europe traveled to Rome to receive their crown from Christ's vicar on Earth –

worldly authority flowed from God through the Church and to the secular authorities; the Senate became the Curia; even the word *basilica*, a Latin word now referring to certain major churches, originally meant a Roman public court building. From the fall of Rome to the Renaissance, the knowledge of Rome was preserved by the Church in its libraries, hand-copied by its monks; science during this period, however limited, was conducted by those same monks, and much of Europe's greatest art and architecture was commissioned by the Church. It's not an exaggeration to say that Western Civilization as we know it exists because of the Roman Catholic Church.

The more I learned about the Church, the more I appreciated my Catholic background as a cultural legacy. It wasn't a restoration of faith but an appreciation of heritage. The Church meant something to me after all. Still, I couldn't get past the fact that I did not experience faith in a loving God. As I prepared for the Camino and people asked me why I was going, I mostly demurred, but yes, I did hope that on the Camino I would find faith.

I prayed on the Camino. And I hadn't prayed in a long time. I prayed on my knees. I went to Mass, and I was moved. Almost to tears I was moved. I had forgotten the simple rituals of that communal act. I did not leave Santiago with an instant faith, but I left with a seed of faith.

After I returned from my first Camino, I contacted one of my old theology teachers. We were discussing the reliquary in Santiago, and this teacher said to me, "There's a difference between what we know and what we tell ourselves."

Why hadn't I thought of that? Why hadn't it occurred to me that a literal understanding of religion is not the only valuable understanding of religion? Why hadn't it been obvious to me that a lack of appreciation for one form or aspect of a religion does not negate all other forms and aspects? For my entire life, I was so caught up in a literal interpretation of God, in a literal interpretation of religion, in a literal interpretation of Catholic theology that I quite missed the point.

In that brief conversation, I found a faith I could have, and a faith I could practice, and a place in the Church where I could practice it. The seed of faith that I took from Santiago, or perhaps was given to me by Santiago, continues to grow in me. I continue to desire and strive for a fuller faith in a loving God. I am at home in the Church once again.

I went to Santiago seeking faith, and I found just enough to get me started.

I got the sense talking to many pilgrims that they too were searching for something greater than themselves on their Camino. I think that's what most people mean when they say they are undertaking the journey for spiritual reasons. This aspect of the Camino, related to but less appreciated than the Catholic underpinnings of the ritual, is its humanism.

Modern life, particularly in America, is isolating. We just don't connect with people anymore; there is less a sense of community. A lot of people blame this on technology, and while that plays a role, sociologists noted this shift in western culture well before the Internet and mobile devices became commonplace. People give too much emphasis to unfounded nostalgia, but in general, the sense of community that prevailed for most of human history – the sense that we are all in this together, from raising our kids to participating in global affairs – isn't what it used to be. Where once it was difficult for a person to disavow their community and for their community to disavow them, it's easy today to decide that you are no longer a part of your community, and it's easy for communities to decide who is and isn't a member.

Cause and consequence of this change is that we have fewer and fewer rituals. Rituals are something that communities design and participate in; as the community evolves, so too does the ritual. Rituals help to ground people: "It's harvest time, we're having a harvest festival, and I will contribute to it and participate in it because I am a member of this community." Individuals have rituals too: "It's a weekday morning, and before I deal with anyone else's problems, I'm enjoying this cup of coffee because in this community of one, that's how we start our day."

The Camino is a ritual, and like all rituals, it's grounded in a succession of communities: the pilgrim community, the European community, the Western community, the Christian community, the

Human community. So much of our lives today is about defining ourselves in ways that capture just one part of who we are. I'm a statistician, but that's not who I am. I'm someone's son, but that's not who I am. I want to be someone's husband one day, but that won't be entirely who I am. We all know that to be true – I'm far from the first to say it – but it's one of those things that's easier to know than it is to live. To my mind, the underappreciated humanistic aspect of the Camino ritual is to say: "I'm Ryan, and I'm walking this road because I am a member of the community of the human race." It's a ritual that captures its participants in their totality in a way that little else does.

When we think back upon the millions of pilgrims who have walked the road to Santiago, they are anonymous to us, but we recognize, however faintly, that they were human beings who belonged somewhere, and by their undertaking they became part of a collective history. By walking the road, we declare that we too are human beings, and we too belong somewhere, and we become part of that history.

In a time when it's easier to decide where we don't belong, it's a wonderful moment in life when you can decide where we do belong.

Anyway, those are the reasons I walk the Camino. I hope you take the time to consider your motivations, even after your journey.

Part II

Logistics of the Camino

4. Traveling to and from the Camino

When to go

For most people, the unfortunate answer to the question *When should you go on the Camino* is *Whenever you have the time*. If you do have a choice, then here are some things to consider.

June, July, and August are peak tourist season generally as well as the busiest and hottest months of the year on the Camino. Transportation and hotels will be more expensive, and traditional sights and the Camino will be more crowded. On the upside, all the *albergues* are open. On the downside, they're at capacity. With the explosion of interest in the Camino over the past fifteen or so years, there has been an explosion of *albergues* to meet the needs of so many more pilgrims, but it is still possible to find yourself having to hustle to find a bed for the night. That said, churches and schools are often opened up to meet the overflow, and sleeping outside under the stars can be another part of the adventure. Few have to do that, but a few actually prefer to.

July 25th is the feast day of Saint James, so a lot of pilgrims begin their journey so as to arrive in Santiago on the 25th. If the 25th falls on a Sunday, then that is considered a holy year, and a special dispensation is granted to pilgrims who complete their pilgrimage in such a year. As crowded as non-holy years can be in July, holy years are doubly so. But the 25th is a public holiday in Galicia, and the celebration in Santiago is an immense world experience. The Pope has been known to make the occasional live address.

April, May, September, and October are the shoulder season months. These are less crowed and less expensive. The weather is still pleasant, though it can be rainy in the Spring (in Galicia especially, but the weather is usually damp there). Even into late September, the temperatures can still be hot. I consider this an ideal time to go, as the weather is more pleasant than the summer months, *albergues* and bars are still open, and it's a little less crowded.

November, December, January, February, and March are the off-season. This is the cheapest and least crowded time of year to go, but the weather can be cold and wet, and because there is less pilgrim traffic, many *albergues* and bars shut down for the season. In addition, the cold temperatures require a little more gear, and thus add to the cost. But because these are the off-season months, airfare, train tickets, and accommodation prices can be lower than in peak and shoulder seasons, so the expense of additional gear may be a wash.

You can find temperature and precipitation tables at the American Pilgrims on the Camino website.

Getting to Europe

It's important to remember when making all of your arrangements that most flights land in Europe the day AFTER you take off, so if you leave on Thursday you arrive on Friday. You may think it's obvious, but people do make that mistake.

Jet lag is real but perhaps overblown. At least some folks are more susceptible to it than others, but you can fight it, and staying active is the best way to fight jet lag. After you land and get settled, go for a walk. Fresh air and sunshine are the best remedies for jet lag, as is staying hydrated. My goal on my first day is to go to bed between 9:00 and 10:00 after a full day of activity.

A flight from the US to Europe costs from $1,100 to $1,800 dollars for an economy seat and takes from seven to twelve hours depending on where you take off from and where you land.

Direct from JFK to Madrid is the shortest flight to Spain that I know of. The seats on transatlantic flights are a bit larger than on a domestic flight, and on the newer planes there's a TV screen built into the seat in front of you with a menu of movies, and there's often an outlet to charge your devices between the seats. Most people don't like flying, but transatlantic flights are not as bad as you may think.

It takes a lot of frequent flyer miles to fly to Europe, but if you have them and have some flexibility, it saves you a lot of money. The catch is that flying with miles limits your travel dates and destinations. Of course business and first class cost more miles, but they limit you in other ways too. Here's how:

- A rewards flight costs a certain number of miles, but that number changes depending on the date. It will cost more miles to fly on a Friday or Saturday than on a Thursday or Monday. Similarly, flights in peak seasons or near holidays cost more miles.
- Not all flights have seats for rewards travel, so if you see a flight you like, it might not be available to you. The flights that are available tend to be less desirable. For instance, you want the 2:20pm to your connection city to shorten your layover, but the available awards flight leaves at 6:00am, turning your short layover into a day of sitting in an airport wishing you were a tree.
- Rewards flights tend to go only to major airports. For instance, at least on American Airlines (and partners), you can't fly into or out of Santiago on miles. Even major tourist cities and national capitals may not be reachable via miles. I found out that American Airlines doesn't have rewards flights into Lisbon, Venice, or Ljubljana, at least when I've checked.
- You can't pay for part of a flight in miles and the rest in cash anymore. It's one or the other. Perhaps you are close to your rewards ticket. You can buy more miles, or a friend can gift them to you, but with that comes a hefty fee (the more miles, the more dollars). I looked into it once and found that buying some additional miles and transferring some from a friend would have cost more than paying cash *and* would have limited my travel options to boot.

I've flown to Europe on miles. It took several years of using the airline's credit card to accumulate those miles. I saved about $1,300, and immediately opened a new credit card that just gives me cash rewards. The experience soured me on using miles – you get less cash back than miles, but at least you can actually spend the cash. That's not to say that having an airline credit card isn't useful; you can check a bag for free, board in Group 1, and are more likely to get an upgrade. If you fly for business, it's a great deal: the company or client reimburses you for the flight, but you get the perks and miles.

The class upgrades that you can purchase are generally not useable on international flights, but it never hurts to ask for an upgrade just because (the worst they can say is no). Call the airline a few weeks before your flight and ask, and again a day before you leave. You can ask at the airport, but I've found that unless you are a Platinum Power Ranger Awards Member, you won't get one at the gate. I asked for an upgrade once, and the woman at the gate apologetically told me it would cost another $3,200 dollars. I replied that that wasn't an upgrade: it's buying a more expensive ticket. But from my seat in coach I could at least see the much more comfortable seats in first class that recline completely flat. They were all empty, so I got a great look.

Choose your seats carefully. Some of the features that seem nice on a domestic flight can be worse on a transatlantic flight. For instance, an exit or bulkhead seat's tray table is stored in the arm of the seat, which gives you less room side-to-side and makes the tray a tight fit if you're a bigger person. You can look up the best seats on a given aircraft at various websites, including seatguru.com.

When booking your flights, pay attention to how long your layovers are. Some of them can be very long, and some of them can be so short that you'll have a hard time making it to your next flight, especially in large airports where the gates may be far apart, if you have to change terminals, and yes, even if you have to change airports (which does happen in cities with multiple airports, such as New York).

You will have to go through customs on your way home, something to keep in mind if you're checking any luggage and your connection is tight.

Should you schedule some time for traditional sightseeing?

Yes! If you have the time and money. I'm of the opinion that if you're flying all the way to Europe, you'd be foolish not to spend at least one day doing some traditional sightseeing. I'm a sucker for

European culture, so it doesn't take much for me to come up with an excuse to spend a day seeing major sights. If you take your pilgrim's mindset to the major cities, you can do it cheaply, too: walk instead of using taxis or public transit, and stay in hostels (they're not just for students anymore). Coming from the US, chances are that to get to a smaller city, like Pamplona, Santiago, or Bayonne, you'll have a layover in Madrid, London, or Paris. Consider taking a day to enjoy those cities' sights before heading for the Camino, or choose any other city you can get a cheap flight out of to your destination.

My first Camino was my first trip to Europe, and my goal was to spend a day in Madrid on the front end and a day in Rome on the back end. I couldn't make Rome work, but my flight into Madrid landed at 6:30 in the morning, I dropped my bag off at my hostel, oriented myself, and saw the Puerto del sol, Plaza Mayor, the Reina Sofia Museum, the Prado Museum, took a brief nap back at my hostel, saw the Royal Palace, caught the last few minutes of Mass at the Almundena Cathedral next door, had some *churros con chocolate* at *Chocolateria San Gines*, and had some *patatas bravas* with a new friend staying in my hostel. Tired? Yes, but I crossed the palace off my list of things to see in life, saw the greatest painting by arguably the greatest painter of the 20th century (Picasso's *Guernica* at the Reina Sofia), and saw a couple masterpieces at the Prado (where *Las Meninas*, which some experts regard as the greatest painting ever created, hangs). I was on my way to the Camino by noon the next day. I managed all of that by buying and reading a good Spain travel guidebook that gave me the tricks on avoiding lines – Rick Steves' Spain guidebook. The only blister I got on that trip I got in Madrid, walking several miles around the old part of the city in my non-hiking socks.

With the cheap flights within Europe and the efficient rail system, it is possible to spend a day in another country, travel to the Camino the next day, and start your walk the day after (or immediately if you arrive early), making traditional sightseeing on a Camino trip easier and less expensive than you might think. Easyjet and RyanAir are the cheapest airlines in Europe (as cheap as €20 for a flight), but beware of the add-on charges. These airlines serve smaller cities and airports, something to pay attention to (i.e., your flight to London lands at a smaller airport far outside the city).

Getting to the Camino

Note that major cities often have more than one train station and bus station. For that matter, they can have more than one airport. Sometimes these stations and airports are quite a ways from the city center. When purchasing tickets, making connections, and booking accommodations, be sure you're going to the right station. If you arrive at Chamartin train station in Madrid but you're actually leaving from Atocha station in Madrid, you have a haul to get to you're your train and might not make it.

By far the most popular Camino starting points are Sarria and Saint Jean Pied de Port. The former is the last town on the Camino Frances from which you can start and still receive your compostela. It is 111km from Santiago. Saint Jean Pied de Port (SJPP) is the traditional starting point for the Camino Frances and is 790km from Santiago.

I've seen some Camino narrative authors use the term "jumpers" or make other disparaging remarks to describe pilgrims who start further down the Camino, such as at Sarria, than the absolute terminus of any particular route, such as SJPP (which technically is not the terminus of that route). I have nothing but respect for people who walk the entire Camino, and I know that most of them don't have an issue with those who can only walk part of it. To those who do have an issue, I say piss off! Not everyone has the time or financial resources to take an entire month off to walk the entire Camino, though many badly want to. Many people who don't have enough time to walk the entire route in one go start at SJPP, walk as far as they can in the time they have, and then return the following year to pick up where they left off. Others start at Sarria. These people are not jumpers – they are pilgrims.

As the Camino Frances is the route with which I have experience, it is where I will offer detailed advice. If you plan on another route, your daily Camino guidebook and online Camino forums are the best places to learn how to get to your starting point.

Getting to Sarria

From Madrid, you can catch a RENFE (Spain's national railway) train to Sarria. In 2016, there were two trains in high pilgrim season, one during the day that taking six hours and costing $65 for a second-class seat, and an overnight that took 8 hours and was also $65. First-class seats are $85 on the day train, $190 on the overnight train, and a sleeping berth on the overnight is $275.[1] If you take the day train, plan on getting started the next day. The night train arrives at 7:00am, so you can either get started that day, or if you like, you can hang around Sarria (but there's not much to see).

Santiago has its own airport, so you can fly into Santiago and catch a train or bus to Sarria (or starting points in Portugal such as Tuy and Porto). The bus schedules tend to be seasonal, and there are taxi and shuttle services available as well, though these are more expensive. If you can find three friends to share the taxi, it might be a good price, though.

You can buy train and bus tickets in Europe at the station without fear of getting gouged on price like with a last minute airline ticket. That said, I like to purchase in advance so I know there are seats available for the trip I want, and to help me plan my time. You can purchase RENFE tickets 60 days in advance. It varies with bus tickets by the company. Raileurope.com and petrabax.com are more useable for viewing schedules and purchasing tickets than the official RENFE website.

Note when using calendars on Spanish websites that their week starts on Monday, so pay attention to the date to ensure you don't show up on a Saturday with a ticket for Sunday.

Getting to Saint Jean Pied de Port

You can get to SJPP from either the French side of the Pyrenees or the Spanish side. Neither one is direct.

---

[1] Prices may change in 2017.

From the Spanish side, the easiest way is to get to Pamplona. You can fly there with connections through a major city, or you can fly into any major city in Spain and catch a train if you want to do some sightseeing. A train from Madrid to Pamplona is about $70. From Pamplona, there are daily buses to SJPP as well as shuttle services. Again, these services are cheaper if you share them with others.

The long-distance buses in Spain are run by private companies and are unique to the region. Unlike trains in Europe, there is no single website for viewing bus schedules. You'll need to check the bus company websites. Conda.es is one of them. The bus schedules for Pamplona to SJPP are seasonal, the trip takes about two hours, and it costs less than €20. Unfortunately, bus company websites are often in Spanish only and can be difficult to use; refer to a Camino forum for the most up to date information on the best bus options. In whatever city you are making your connection, you can also simply arrive and go straight to the tourist information office or bus station and ask what bus takes you to SJPP.

Since the bus from Pamplona to SJPP takes two hours, you probably want to take an early-afternoon bus to be sure you get to SJPP early enough to get a bed if you're traveling in high season. That's something to keep in mind when figuring out how, and at what time, you'll get to Pamplona or wherever your connection is.

From France, you can fly into Bayonne via Paris, then catch a train to Biarritz, then another train from Biarritz to SJPP.

Money on the Camino

Cash is king on the Camino and for tourists in Europe in general. I'm no different than most Americans in that I use my credit and debit cards for almost every purchase at home, no matter how small. I never saw anyone use a credit card on the Camino, and many bars and albergues don't accept them. It's also not uncommon for hotels and restaurants that do accept credit cards to charge an additional fee for them, and in addition to the exchange rate, your credit card company may charge you an international transaction fee as well. The credit card system is also different in Europe, and you'll need to know your pin, if you don't already (that's right – credit cards have pins like debit cards, and that's what they use in Europe instead of signing receipts). Using cash makes things so much easier.

Also, no one uses traveler's checks anymore. There are fees to get them, fees to cash them, and the hassle and time of waiting to get and cash them.

Anyone changing money is also making money. Whether it's a bank, ATM, or a store, they charge a little for themselves in the transaction, or offer a lower exchange rate and pocket the difference. Banks, especially in the US, and stores in Europe charge more than ATMs, so use ATMs.

You can use a debit card or a credit card to get cash from an ATM. With a debit card, you will pay a flat transaction fee, a few dollars, that doesn't get higher even if you take out more money. You can minimize these fees by minimizing your trips to the ATM, which means taking out the maximum amount your bank will allow. You will need your pin to withdraw money, so memorize it in advance and don't write it down and stick it in your wallet.

If you withdraw cash from an ATM using your credit card, your bank will treat the transaction as a cash advance, a short-term loan which comes with a high interest rate. Using your debit card just withdraws your money from your bank account, so there is no interest. If your checking account does not have a debit card attached to it, get one before you go to Europe and memorize the pin.

Most of Europe uses the chip-and-pin type of credit and debit cards. These cards, instead of a magnetic strip, have a microchip embedded in them, and instead of signing the receipt, you enter your pin number. In most places in Europe, you can still use your magnetic strip card, and if you have a problem using one at an ATM or kiosk (such as in a train station), the teller or ticket agent at the counter can run your card for you.

It used to be that if you wanted a chip-and-pin card in the US you had to specifically ask for one, and it came with a high annual fee. But since October 2015, new federal regulations are require banks and credit card companies to switch to a chip system because the chip is more secure than the magnetic strip – everyone will have a chip-and-pin card soon.

Before you travel, call your credit card companies and/or bank to let them know where you'll be traveling and when. Be sure to include any place you have a layover. This prevents the bank or credit card company's system from thinking your transactions are fraudulent and stopping them. If your card throws up a red flag, you'll need to call the bank to unlock your card, and that's a real pain when you're calling from Europe, especially if you don't have your phone set to call in Europe. Avoid even the chance of that happening – call ahead before you leave the US. When you do, find out what the daily or transaction maximum is for withdrawing cash using your debt card, and request that it be increased if you think you'll need to withdraw more. You can also ask for an increase in your credit limit from your credit card company. Note that some banks treat the weekend as a single day, so the daily withdrawal limit will apply to the entire weekend.

Use calling your bank as a reminder to get on the State Department's website and register your travel. I don't like the idea of the government keeping tabs on my whereabouts more than anybody else, but in the (very) unlikely event of an issue wherever it is I'm traveling, the nearest consulate or embassy knows I'm there and won't forget me when the helicopters are pulling folks off the roof.

The Camino is probably the cheapest trip you will ever take other than camping. Twenty-five euros a day can be more than sufficient depending on where you sleep and what you eat. ATMs are easy to find in the major cities. The first thing I do after getting my baggage at the airport when traveling abroad is find an ATM. As of this writing, 1 euro is approximately $1.10 (the best it's been in a long time). A quick Google search can give you the latest conversion rate.

I take my debit card, my Visa credit card, and my American Express credit card. Two credit cards might be considered overkill by some, but I like the mental security of having a backup, and some places won't accept certain brands of credit or debit card. In addition, you should take $150 of American cash as a true emergency fund. It's not a bad idea to know the location of a Western Union in some of the major cities you'll be traveling through in case you need someone to wire money to you.

The worst happens and your money belt, along with your passport, cash, credit card, and debit card, is lost or stolen. Don't panic. Start by canceling your credit and debit cards, then get to a US consulate or embassy. They will be able to get you a new passport and will give you a short-term loan to get you back on your feet. Your general European travel guidebook should contain more information on this unlikely problem.

On the last day of your trip, you don't have to spend all the euros you have left. Major airports, like the one you're flying to to get home or have a layover in, have currency exchange shops that will turn your euros back into dollars. Often these are in the domestic as well as international terminals. Yes, you will lose a little in the transaction, but dollars are more valuable than the chintzy souvenirs you only bought to spend the money.

The language barrier

What do native English speakers and native Spanish speakers have in common? They both seem to think that if only they talk louder and more slowly, they can make people understand. Seriously, having someone ramble on at me in Spanish even after I've said (in Spanish) that I don't speak Spanish was an eye opening experience. It's instant appreciation for what non-English speakers go through when talking to us (for instance, you'll find that no matter how slowly someone speaks in a foreign language, it still sounds very fast to you, which doesn't matter because you don't understand it at any speed).

While Europe is multilingual, the Spanish and Portuguese are known for being the least multilingual countries in Western Europe. That isn't universally true, of course. Throughout Europe, young people and urbanites are more likely to speak multiple languages, and English has become the second language of choice for most Europeans. On the Camino, however, you're passing through mostly rural communities with many older residents. Despite the international crowd of pilgrims, many of the locals you will meet speak only Spanish or just a few words of English. But I only speak English, and it wasn't an issue at all.

Communication with limited language can even be part of the fun. You will be doing just a few things on the Camino: walking, eating, and sleeping. You don't need many words to manage those things, and you'd be surprised by how many Spanish words you've picked up from pop culture (and some of them aren't even dirty).

While the Spanish may be, relatively speaking, monolingual, the country is multilingual. They speak Catalan in Cataluña, Euskara (also called Basque) in Navarra, Gallego in Galicia, and Castillian – what we consider Spanish – everywhere. Spaniards who speak one of these regional languages at home speak Spanish as well. The late Spanish dictator, Francisco Franco, wanted to eliminate these languages and cultures to stamp out the independence movements in those regions, but these small languages and cultures are thriving again. You will pass through Navarra and Galicia, and while I don't recommend you try to learn every word you can in their languages, I find it helpful and polite to learn a handful of words for those areas in addition to more words in Spanish. Remember that you are in their country; they are doing you a favor by speaking in English, so return the favor by learning a handful of their words.

Spanish is a gendered language. In general, words ending in –a are female, and words ending in –o are male. Masculine nouns are preceded by uno or el as in (uno/el tren = a/the train). Feminine nouns are preceded by una or la (una/la casa = a/the house). The plural of el is los, and the plural of la is las. If a word doesn't end in –o or –a, then look to the article (un/una or el/la) to know the gender. There are more than a few complications to these rules, but for the traveller, this is sufficient.

In certain parts of Spain, the letters c and z are pronounced like our th-. For instance, Barcelona is not pronounced Bar-suh-lona; it's pronounced Bar-thuh-lona.

Plurals in Spanish are made the same way as in English, by adding –s or –es to the end.

A quick Google search can lead you to websites with plenty of information on Spanish grammar, conjugation, and more vocabulary if you're interested. The appendix contains some important words and phrases for the Camino, but here are some tips for making communication easier.

Start a conversation by asking if the person you're talking to speaks English (ask them in their language!). If they say no, try to speak in the native language of whomever you're talking to. Sometimes after a few words, they'll start trying out their limited (or sometimes not so limited) English to help you out.

If they do speak English, speak slowly, annunciate, avoid colloquial language, and don't use idioms.

If they don't speak English, do your best in their language. If someone can speak grammatically incorrect, poorly pronounced English and be understood by English speakers, you can do the same in Spanish.

Gestures work. Pointing works. Sometimes writing something down or drawing a picture works. Do whatever you need to do to communicate, and don't be embarrassed. It's all part of the experience.

Pilgrims are truly international, and the younger ones almost all speak some English. As Europe's economies integrate, many young people look for work across the continent, and the language the continent has in common is English. You'll meet pilgrims from all over Europe and the world. Germany was well represented on my trip, as were the Low Countries, Sweden, and Italy. No, you don't have to learn their words too. You'll also meet plenty of British, Irish, and other Americans.

If you are travelling through France, the same rules apply when it comes to learning some French words, but if you're only going to be in France for a day or so, for instance if you're just spending the night in Saint Jean before heading out, you'll do just fine with a couple words. If you detect an undercurrent of condescension when a French person lowers themselves to speak in our guttural Germanic language, don't take it personally. To the French, their language is their greatest art.

Most importantly, your mother was 100% correct when she told you that you can get almost anything you need in life with *"por favor"* and *"gracias."*

Measurements, numbers, and time on the Camino

Spain uses the metric system, the Celsius scale and the twenty-four-hour clock. All three are easy to master.

For measuring weight, the metric system uses grams. There are one thousand grams in a kilogram (kilo). One kilogram is 2.2 pounds, so half a kilo is about one pound, a quarter kilo is about half a pound, etc. One hundred grams of lunchmeat is a little less than a quarter pound, or a decent sandwich.

For measuring volume, the metric system uses liters. One liter is approximately 34 ounces, so a 32-ounce Nalgene bottle is about one liter, half a liter is about 16 ounces, two liters is about 64 ounces, and 4 liters is approximately a gallon. One liter of water weighs 1 kilogram (how many pounds is that? 2.2).

For measuring long distance, the metric system uses kilometers. One kilometer is about 0.6 miles, give or take. Five kilometers is about three miles. To do a quick conversion from kilometers to miles, divide the kilometers by half and then add back ten percent of the original (e.g., 1 kilometer divided by 2 is 0.5; 10% of 1 is 0.1; 0.5 plus 0.1 is 0.6, the number of miles in a kilometer). You may find as you hike that kilometers are a little easier to judge than miles.

For temperature, Europeans uses the Celsius scale. The actual conversion from Celsius to Fahrenheit is to divide the Celsius temperature by 5, then multiply by 9, then add 30. To ballpark the conversion from Celsius to Fahrenheit, just double the Celsius and add 30. So 20 degrees Celsius is 70 degrees Fahrenheit, a comfortable day.

Decimals are different in Europe. Instead of a period, they use a comma. So where as a Euro and a half for us is €1.50, in Europe it's €1,50. By the same token, whereas we would put a comma in a four-digit number (there are 5,280 feet in a mile), in Europe they use a decimal (there are 5.280 feet in a mile).

In Europe, the first floor of a building is the ground floor, and what we call the second floor is the first floor.

The twenty-four-hour clock (better known at the military clock in the US) is easy to use. Any time before 1:00pm is the same as on the twelve-hour clock, except between midnight and 1:00am. For instance, 12:30am is expressed as 00:30. Anytime after 12:59pm, just add 12. So 1:00pm becomes 13:00, 5:30pm becomes 17:30.

Returning from the Camino

If you're tackling the whole Camino, getting out of Santiago is easy. Santiago has an airport with flights to Madrid and a few other major cities, as well as a train station. The simplest thing you can do to make your trip out easy is not fly out of the same city that you flew into. To do this, instead of selecting "round trip," select "multiple destinations" when you buy your plane ticket online. I've heard of pilgrims, usually Americans who are not accustomed to international travel, flying into Bayonne, starting at SJPP, walking to Santiago, and then taking trains all the way back to Bayonne to fly out again. They could have just flown out of Santiago.

If you're only doing a section of the Camino, you'll most likely need to rely on a bus to get you back to a transportation hub. Pamplona, Burgos, and Leon are all major cities with small airports and medium train stations, and trains do stop in smaller towns as well. Figure out how to get back before you leave. If you're going to be ending your trip in a small town, you'll probably take a bus to the nearest train station and then catch a train to wherever you're flying out of, and that will likely all need to happen the day before your flight. Save yourself the stress, and potentially missed flight, and plan ahead.

Hiring guide companies

It is entirely possible for any person in reasonable shape, at any age, to walk the Camino solo. Thousands of people do so every year.

Many go with friends. You also have the option of hiring a guide company for either a guided tour or for a self-guided tour.

In either case, the guide company will make the logistical arrangements for you. In the case of a guided tour, this typically includes transporting your luggage from hotel to hotel, so you hike with just a daypack. Your guide will know (or at least should know) the history of the places you are passing through and will have some expertise in religion, art, and architecture to enrich your experience. You will travel with a group, and these groups can be either completely *ad hoc*, or they can be arranged around a common trait (seniors, for instance) or interest (religion).

Self-guided tours typically make only the hotel arrangements, but some of these might include luggage transport as well. Some companies may also provide you with some information on the places through which you pass, but other than that, you walk on your own.

Whether you hire a guide company or not, you can hire a service (if one is locally available, and there usually is), to transport your bag to your next *albergue*. You (or the service) can call ahead to the *albergue*. If you do this, it's important to take a daypack so that you can carry the essentials (e.g. extra socks, first aid kit, water).

I chose not to use a guide company. Tour groups can be excellent travel, but I wasn't worried about making my own arrangements or getting lost (nearly impossible on the Camino), and tour groups can also be somewhat insulating, and I wanted to meet new people and have new experiences. That said, tours offer (hopefully) good company, and a good guide can create an incredible experience for guests by providing historical, artistic, and religious insights about the areas the Camino passes through.

There are plenty of *albergues* to stay at along the Camino and few of them accept reservations. The only advantage I can see to self-guided tours on the Camino is if you want to stay in hotels and are willing to trade some freedom for some convenience. I liked being able to stop wherever and whenever I decided I was done for the day, but if that's not your personality, then self-guided tours can take a logistical burden off your shoulders.

About sending your backpack ahead. Some people consider this cheating. I don't. First, for people who may not be able to carry a pack, sending their luggage ahead enables them to do the Camino, and however you do it, the Camino is worth doing. Second, the weight of a backpack is not the primary source of discomfort on the Camino; the distance is. Carrying yourself to Santiago is the real challenge, physically and mentally. If you need to send your pack ahead, or just want to, do it and be confident that you are still a pilgrim.

I did my Camino solo, without a guide, made my own logistical arrangements, and carried my pack. That's the perspective of the rest of this book.

5. The daily Camino

What I like about hiking is how singular it is. In our modern lives, it seems we rarely have the chance to focus on just one thing, but when I'm out on the trail, my world shrinks down to my immediate surroundings and my body. After the first few miles, I fall into a rhythm and just keep going. I imagine myself as the Energizer Bunny, moving slowly but inexorably forward, confident that my feet will take me all the places I wish to go. It is a source of pleasure and confidence and security.

The activity of hiking and the daily routine of long distance hiking have that in common. It's about repetition, and somehow while most repetitive tasks in our lives bore us and make us feel trapped, the repetitions of the hike make us feel free.

Even on long hikes that turn into forced marches, the pain I sometimes experience becomes its own Zen task: my world shrinks down even more, until it is just me and the pain. A lot of people will never understand it, but I think Jon Krakauer said it best in his book about the 1996 Everest disaster:

> "People who don't climb mountains...tend to assume that the sport is a reckless, Dionysian pursuit of ever escalating thrills. But the notion that climbers are merely adrenaline junkies chasing a righteous fix is a fallacy...Above the comforts of Base Camp...the ratio of misery to pleasure was greater by an order of magnitude than any other mountain I'd been on...And in subjecting ourselves to week after week of toil, tedium, and suffering, it struck me that most of us were probably seeking, above all else, something like a state of grace."

Of course, what Krakauer was doing up on Everest is a whole different animal, but hiking is like any other physical undertaking, by turns exhilarating and exhausting. Read any memoir of a long distance hiker, and you'll find that most of them at some point compare the task of long distance hiking to a job. It is not all warm days, cool breezes, and fields of wildflowers; some days it is mud and cold and stubbed toes. When I think back on my Camino journey and all my days on the trail, I think I cherish the hard days most, for I felt a greater sense of accomplishment at the end of them.

What time should you start hiking every day?

What time do you want/need to start hiking every day is the better question. *Albergues* generally ask guests to leave by 8am so they can start cleaning up for the next group of pilgrims, so expect to leave your albergue no later than 8. Whether you start hiking or spend more time lingering over breakfast is up to you, but there are some things to consider.

First, how fast do you hike? You should have a general idea based on your practice hikes. Personally, I'm a very slow hiker.

Second, when do you want to arrive? One of my favorite things about the Camino is not needing to know this answer to a certainty. The answer *Until I stop* is liberating. But even if you don't know exactly when or where, having a ballpark helps.

I know I'm a slow hiker, and I know that I like to arrive in the early part of the afternoon so I can spend it napping, having lunch, doing chores, and exploring, so I leave my *albergue* before 7am.

On the trail

You'll find that many pilgrims like to get a few miles under their belt before stopping for breakfast. Cafes along the Camino are busy in the morning, with one line at the counter and another at the restroom. You're not on a schedule! Try to linger. I've found that other pilgrims are especially sociable in the morning: they've done some miles and are still feeling fresh.

Most daily Camino guidebooks break down the Way into 12- to 15-mile segments, though some are longer and some are shorter. You can make any day longer or shorter, though, as you pass through villages where you can cut a day short, or hike on a little further to the next village. Good guidebooks list all of these villages.

The terrain on the Camino is varied. If you start at Saint Jean Pied de Port, your first day is actually the hardest: up one side of the Pyrenees Mountains and down the other. It's one of the longer days, but if you book in advance, you can cut the day in half by staying at Refuge Orisson (at the time of this writing the only stopping point between SJPP in France and Roncesvalles in Spain; €35 for a bed, dinner, and breakfast).

The terrain gets flatter as you move west onto the Meseta, Spain's high, flat plain between Burgos and Leon. From Leon, you begin to ascend again into the Galician Mountains. These are not high mountains, but they are formidable. Flat ground is of course the easiest topography to hike on. Uphill is hardest on the lungs but soft on the feet (shorter steps mean less force on impact), while downhill is hardest on the joints.

Some people compare the physical Camino to the spiritual Camino. Early on, the walking is hard (up the Pyrenees and down the other side), and one walks slowly, struggling with their motivations and getting used to a new way of living. In the next stage, the walking becomes easier (the flatness of the Meseta), and you gain confidence, absorbing the experience while continuing to contemplate your journey. In the final stage, the walk becomes slightly more difficult again (as you ascend into the Galician mountains), but you are used to it; the struggle instead is with the coming end of the journey and the realization that you must leave the Camino, return to your everyday life, and take whatever wisdom you can carry home with you.

One could say something similar of the daily walk. The first few hours are spent loosening muscles and warming up. It takes a while to hit a consistent stride. About halfway through the day, rhythm and endorphins kick in, and your stride becomes fairly consistent. Finally, as you near your destination, you start to slow and struggle a bit more as the exertion of the day takes its toll and those endorphins that have kept the discomfort down dry up. It's always the first few miles and the last few that are the hardest, but ultimately they are the most memorable.

The path itself

The actual pathway varies every day. Parts of the Camino are over Roman roads. Gravel and crushed stone are common. Parts of the Camino are over and alongside highways, or down village roads. Particularly in Galicia, you will find stretches where it is impossible to not step on cow flops (aim for the dry ones). I find that no surface is more comfortable to walk on than God's own dirt, but a flat road is my second choice. Most hikers average two to three miles per hour during the course of a 15-mile hike over varied terrain.

Navigating the Camino is pretty easy. Scallop shells and yellow arrows point the way, painted on the road, trees, or buildings; embedded in stone markers; or on signs secured to posts or trees. The Camino is probably the best-marked trail in the world. It is possible to take a wrong turn, but it's hard to stay lost, as you won't see any shells or arrows. Turn around and backtrack, look at the map in your guidebook, read the route description, or ask a local to direct you back to the path.

How your hike goes depends largely on your likes and dislikes. Sometimes you'll hike with other people, sometimes you won't. Some people take a music player on the Camino, some don't. Some take a camera, some don't. There's no right way to do the Camino, and that's the point: you get to do it entirely your way.

Arriving at your destination

Whether you stop for lunch is more dependent on what time you get started and what time you intend to arrive at your destination.

I like to stop for the day around two in the afternoon, so I skip lunch on the trail.

I recommend scoping out an albergue or hotel as soon as you arrive at your destination. Ask fellow pilgrims, refer to your guidebook, or just look for signs. If one is full, another is probably a few doors further down the street. After getting your credencial stamped at the front desk and turning over a few euros, pick a bed in the dorm or go to your assigned room. Resist the temptation to take a nap. In fact, if you can avoid it, don't even sit down, lest you find a you-shaped sweat stain on the sheets when you get back up. Shower stalls and hot water are in short supply (lo, how much we suffer), so I suggest grabbing your shower kit and cleaning up as soon as you can.

Once you're clean, I suggest doing your laundry (more on this later). Sometimes there's a sink inside, other times outside, but get this chore out of the way early so that everything dries before you go to bed.

Finally, do whatever it is you want to do next. This is my favorite part of the day: after a long hike, I'm clean and relaxed, with my aching feet propped up on a chair, a bottle of wine on the table, and a parade of people from all over the world to keep me entertained. This is an excellent time to keep a journal.

The Spanish siesta is alive and well, especially in rural Spain. It is very common, especially in the early stages of the Camino, to arrive at your destination for the day only to find the bars closed and the hospitaleros are home having their mid-day meal. However, that's not absolutely the case, particularly after Sarria. In any case, the siesta starts around 1pm and ends around 4pm. If you find that you're arriving during siesta and can't find an open bar or albergue, consider stopping for lunch around noon, or remember to carry some food with you, or perhaps adjust your hiking schedule to arrive a little earlier. Or just take part in the siesta – find some shade and relax.

After a nap, it's fun to wander around the albergue or town, looking for interesting sights, old friends, and new friends. Before you know it, it's dinner time.

Evenings

It can be difficult to have dinner by yourself in Europe, and that's a good thing. If you're hiking solo, the empty seats at your café table, especially on the patio, have a way of filling themselves with fellow pilgrims. When abroad, Americans who would never talk to a stranger, yet alone share a table, have a tendency to gravitate toward one another. Europeans, who can be more reserved than Americans in most situations, are used to sharing tables, especially if they're from Scandinavia, Germany, or Austria where communal outdoor restaurants are more common.

Nearly every village has a church, but not every village has a priest. Vocations are down in Europe, dramatically. In one of the great ironies of history, the continent that used to send missionaries to the New World now has New World priests going to Europe to minister to the dwindling number of practicing Christians. However, that's less of an issue in Spain. Pilgrims' Masses in the evenings are common, and I highly recommend them even if you're not Catholic. These are a chance to commune with your fellow pilgrims, consider what has brought you to the Camino, and reflect on our common humanity.

Albergues generally turn off the lights at 10pm. You'll probably be eager to sleep well before that.

6. Eating on the Camino

I'll probably anger a lot of people by saying this, but Spain is not known for its cuisine. At least not in the sense that the Italians, French, and even the Germans are known for theirs. The Spanish decidedly eat to live – the food is nourishing, filling, and it can be inexpensive.

A bar in Spain is a restaurant as well as a place to get a drink. On the Camino, the food typically comes in set portions, but in the major cities, and in some village bars, the dishes come in different sizes. Here's a guide:

- *Pinchos*: small portion, like an hors d'oeuvre.
- *Tapas*: a snack size
- *Racione*: a meal size
- *Media racione*: half a meal

These words aren't universal, though. In Navarre, a *tapas* is a *racione*, for instance. Your waiter can help you avoid ordering too much or too little. Of course, not every dish comes in a particular size.

Breakfast

Like the rest of southern Europe, breakfast in Spain is a light affair. Bread, jam, maybe some fruit or a pastry is what you'll typically get. *Café con leche* is the customary drink. I'm told it's very good, though I'm not a coffee drinker.

Some *albergues* and hotels serve breakfast, but most pilgrims head out the door and stop at a bar further down the Camino for their first meal of the day. These bars tend to be very busy and have a lively morning atmosphere.

Lunch and dinner

Lunch and dinner can be either a simple dish or a three-course meal called alternatively the *menu del dia* or a pilgrim's menu (same thing, but it gets called a pilgrims' menu on the Camino). The pilgrims' menu may pre-date the *menu del dia*, but the latter is ingenuous. The dictator Francisco Franco decreed that every Spaniard should be able to afford one meal a day, so bars were obliged to offer a three-course meal for what comes out to about $12. For that $12, you get a lot. The quality ranges from restaurant to restaurant, but it is fairly consistent on the Camino.

The first course (*primero*) is typically a choice of pasta, salad or soup. On the Camino, expect the pasta to be just spaghetti with canned tomato sauce, most of the time.

The second course (*segundo*) is an entrée usually of chicken or fish. Sometimes there's a beef option, and sometimes ham (more on ham below). French fries come with almost every meal. Expect to eat them almost daily.

Dessert is a pastry, cake, or ice cream.

You have your choice of water or wine with a pilgrims' meal. It's a little odd that you have to pick, but the water is bottled and is sometimes sparkling. You can ask for tap water, but no one will be offended if you just bring your Nalgene bottle to the table, especially in small villages. The wine is almost always red, full-bodied, more fruity than tannic, and you get a full bottle. Wine is cheap in Spain, not surprising since you'll be walking past a lot of vineyards, especially in La Rioja. When I considered my options for a hiking trip this year, that cheap bottle of good wine was a consideration. It's a perfect end to a day on the trail.

There tends to be more variety if you order dishes *al a carte* instead of the pilgrims' menu. That sometimes gets you better food, and sometimes not, but the variety is appreciated. This can include typical Spanish dishes, but also internationalized food as well. Maybe one day you just want a burger. It will probably be a frozen patty that's not even as good as a frozen patty in America, but it's still a burger. I even found chicken nuggets one night. Pizza is common on the Camino, and it's fresh, but as a connoisseur of pizza, I found it seriously lacking. But nonetheless, if you have a hankering for bread, melted cheese, and tomato sauce, it's pizza.

Communal meals

Some albergues, particularly the church-run ones and those on the early stretches of the Camino, offer a communal, family-style meal. It's typically a salad and vegetarian stew. The food is generally good, fills your stomach, and the company fills your soul. Sometimes after these meals, there's some group activity or entertainment.

The quality of the food

For the record, I'm probably a food snob. I'd say the quality of food on the Camino just varies. A lot of food on the Camino is breaded and fried, especially the chicken. I think of it like summer camp or a school cafeteria: frying things makes them easier to produce in quantity. It would be less of an issue if Spain used more sauces and condiments, but I found a lot of the food dry and without recourse to anything to moisten it. I recall in particular a piece of flat, fried chicken and some potato croquets I could have spackled a wall with.

That's not to say it's bad, though. Some meals were just better than others, but don't expect anything memorable on the Camino except in big cities or communal meals. I've found that at least for lunch, when I didn't want a large meal, ordering a tapas-sized dish cost a little more relative to the size of the meal but got me better quality. To be on the safe side, I'd say to expect average and maybe be pleasantly surprised.

Buying and preparing your own food

You can buy food from shops and markets in Spain and prepare your own meal. This tends to be less expensive and provides a break in the monotonous pilgrims' menu. Fresh fruit, bread, cheese, meat, snacks, and canned goods are easy to come by, as is pasta and rice. A picnic lunch on a Spanish hillside is a special experience, and if you bring a little extra you can always invite a passing pilgrim to join you and make a new friend.

Many *albergues* have simple kitchens with simple cooking utensils. You can prepare your own dinner, again a nice break from French fries and canned pasta sauce. I suggest making friends, and you can cook for them one night, and they can cook one of their national dishes another.

Well-known dishes in Spain

Spain may not be known for an overarching cuisine, but it is known for some of it dishes. This is a small sampling of them.

Ham, or *jamon*, is Spain's national dish. They have it on their major holidays and at family gatherings, and in Plaza Mayor in Madrid there is a *Museo del Jamon*, a museum of ham that proves that the world is an okay place. This is not American ham, which is often cut thickly, glazed, and is, in my opinion, spongy and regrettable. Instead, jamon is dry-cured and is served in very thin slices, not unlike Italian prosciutto. It has a firm texture that seems to melt in your mouth. Ham comes in many varieties in Spain; what makes the varieties different is the breed of pig and the manner in which it was raised. *Jamon Iberico* is the most expensive; the pigs were fed only acorns, and the Spanish insist it tastes different than other *jamons*. You'll see *jamons* hanging in bars and restaurants with the hoof still attached.

Paella is a dish of yellow rice, vegetables, seafood, chicken or sausage (often a mix of all of those) flavored with saffron. You'll see the varieties of it advertised on signboards outside restaurants. Most

Spaniards insist that the best paella is found wherever they are from, and Valenica is the dish's birthplace. But if you can find good paella, it's really good.

Patatas bravas are chunks of potato deep-fried and covered with a spicy (*bravas* means "for the brave") yet smooth and creamy sauce. I found them not too spicy. In general, potatoes are frequent enough to be seen as a staple of the Spanish diet, most often fried. This is especially true along the Camino. Really: I hope you like French fries.

Churros are long, thin donuts. They're crunchy on the outside, soft on the inside, and sometimes come with a cup of very thick hot chocolate for dipping (*churros con chocolate*). This is my favorite food in Spain.

Pulpo is especially common in Galicia. I'm not a seafood fan, so it's not really fair for me to judge this dish, but it's prepared pretty simply: take an octopus, beat it with a stick to tenderize it, boil it for a very long time, then snip it into bite size pieces, drizzle it with olive oil, coarse sea salt, sweet and smoky paprika, and serve on a wooden plate with toothpicks. I tried this exactly once, and what I got was a piece of rubbery meat that had no flavor of its own, just olive oil and paprika. That said, many other pilgrims enjoy this dish and say they could eat it every day forever. It's also very nutritious. Maybe I just got it from a bad place. I recommend trying it, and I'll try it again the next time I'm in Galicia, but I also recommend a healthy skepticism as to the edibility of anything that needs to be beaten and boiled and yet is still tough once cooked.

Tortillas in Spain are omelets, built a little like a quiche but not quite the same.

Empanadas are essentially a pie, sometimes fried, of soft dough filled with meat, vegetables, and occasionally cheese. These have become pretty common in the US.

Spain produces a number of cheeses and sausages. Some chorizo (pork-based sausage), a little cheese, and some bread make a great picnic lunch.

Napoleon conquered Spain and made his older brother, Joseph, king in 1808, and the English invaded northern Spain during the Peninsular War to wrest control of Iberia back from the French. We all know that Napoleon's eventual defeat created the national boundaries of modern Europe (with some 20th century adjustments), but most don't know that the English left behind a secret weapon that has terrorized Spain ever since: the *bocadillo*, or sandwich. I love sandwiches; they are my favorite food. The *bocadillo* is a lateral step from the plastic sandwich in my 5-year-old niece's play kitchen. It comes on a piece of long bread, but it's thin, like a sub sandwich that's been shrunk in every dimension. On it is usually a piece of meat that is probably ham (but not the good ham) and a piece of cheese (but not the good cheese). Condiments are nowhere to be seen. You know you're eating some form of sustenance, but it's not food and tastes like something that George Orwell might have said governments would issue in the totalitarian future. Or maybe it tastes like nothing. If you fly on Iberia Airlines, about 90 minutes before your plane lands in Spain they serve you a *bocadillo*, and in your Ambien-induced haze you start to eat it before pausing to wonder why. I'm told the bocadillo can be an excellent sandwich with excellent ingredients and excellent condiments. I didn't find one.

Sherry is a fortified wine (additional alcohol is added to it) from the region of Jerez. Spain produces white and red wine, but red is more common. The wine from the Rioja region is particularly good, but despite ordering by color rather than region or variety (for lack of language skills), I never had a bad glass of wine anywhere in Spain.

Optimizing your dining experience

Particularly in the small villages, the bars are handling a lot of customers. They are making cheap, nutritious, filling food that's easy to produce and meets the tastes of people from all over. A lot of it is frozen or canned. That said, you will get some good food even in these small villages, especially if you take advantage of the communal meals. Anything home cooked is probably better than another meal of underwhelming chicken and frozen French fries. And you can still get good food, especially in the small and large cities, by following a commonsense tip that applies regardless of where you're traveling: eat like the locals.

Anywhere there's more than one restaurant, browse. See what others are eating before you decide where to eat. Look for restaurants away from the main square, where the food may be better, more local, and less expensive. Look for places where the locals are eating, where the menu is small, and where it's in Spanish. The Camino is so international that many if not most bars have menus in several languages, but places that only have a menu in Spanish probably serve local people local food. You're never far from the sea when you're on the Camino, so seafood is always a good bet (if you enjoy it).

When you do eat out, remember that the European dining experience is slow. It's a time to socialize, unwind, and enjoy the sensory experience of eating. Eat like Europeans do, but because slow service is good service, expect to wait, and when you're ready to go, you'll have to ask for the bill. Also, in Europe tips for the wait staff are built into the cost of the meal, so you only need to leave a euro or two on the table. I typically round up, so if my meal is €8,50 and I pay with a €10 note, I leave the change on the table.

It's cheap to eat out on the Camino, but do cook your own meals occasionally, and invite new friends to join you. The two of you will probably make something pretty good. Let a new Italian friend make you some pasta, or throw together your own signature dish from local ingredients.

7. Sleeping on the Camino

You have options on the Camino as to where you sleep, though *albergues* – essentially hostels meant specifically for pilgrims – are the most common option and choice.

It's unfortunately the case, and especially after you reach Sarria, that the Way gets crowded and beds can become scarce in high season. So many more pilgrims are walking the Camino these days. The infrastructure of bars and *albergues* has largely caught up, but yes, it's possible to find yourself having to figure out alternative accommodations. I'll add that sleeping outdoors is not a bad alternative, if you're prepared for it.

Albergues

Albergues are frequent on the Camino and inexpensive. They typically cost less than 10 euros, and many work on a donation basis, particularly in the early stages (if you can afford it, just give the going rate, 5 to 8 euros or so). Many are privately owned, some are operated by monasteries and convents, and some by local and regional governments. They range from comfortable to very Spartan, from small to multistoried buildings, from new to centuries old.

Albergues typically open in the early afternoon, usually no earlier than noon and often as late as three. Particularly in the early and middle stretches of the Camino, the siesta is observed and the *albergue* caretakers (called *hospitaleros*) are at home having their main meal of the day in the late afternoon. They lock the doors and turn out the lights by 10pm, and they boot out any lingering pilgrims by 8am.

To stay in an *albergue*, you will need your *credencial*. The *hospitalero* will stamp your *credencial* and direct you to your room, typically a dormitory full of bunk beds. Some of the dorms are segregated by sex, most of them aren't, and they can have a few beds to several dozen. Privacy is at a premium, so your best bet is to try to arrive on the early side, choose a bed you'll like, spread out your sleeping bag or put your pack on it to "claim" it, and go take a shower. Remember that these are shared facilities, so hot water is limited.

Shower facilities in *albergues* are typically shower stalls, so you do have a modicum of privacy, but these facilities, like the dormitories, are not necessarily segregated by gender. In one *albergue* I stayed in, the bathroom was not connected to the dormitory but was across the entry way and down a hall past the front desk, so there was a parade of people walking from the dorm to the shower in various stages of undress throughout the day.

Europeans have different attitudes toward exposing their bodies, so don't be shocked if you're subjected to a hairy Italian male in skimpy underwear (hey, it happens to all of us). If that makes you uncomfortable, you can stay in hotels, or just learn to live with it. Avert your eyes, or just think of it as one of the cultural quirks that make travel interesting.

Inside the dormitories, be courteous, and that means being quiet. People are napping during the day, and they're tired at night. The dorm is not a place to hang out. Do what you need to in there and then leave. This is especially important if you're starting your Camino farther down the trail; you arrive fresh and ready to go and spend your first night up with friends having a communal meal and laughing it up, but the people who've already been on the Camino for weeks are tired and want to go to bed. Everything echoes in an *albergue*. Don't be one of "those" pilgrims.

You will share the dorms with people who snore, and yes, people do fart in their sleep. You do too in all likelihood. It's just something you have to deal with; it does no good to wake up a snorer or to confront them in the morning. Wear your earplugs if it bothers you.

Albergues all have some sort of laundry facility, even if it's just a sink outside. The clotheslines get full, and while you can make some room for your things, it's not very pilgrim-like to just put someone's dry things on the ground.

There are communal spaces in *albergues*, including lobbies, kitchens, and patios. These are good places to read, talk with friends, and spend your afternoons. The kitchens have basic appliances, pots and pans, and utensils, and sometimes you'll find something left behind by another pilgrim. It's nice to take a break from the pilgrims' menus and cook something fresh, and it's a good opportunity to get to know your fellow pilgrims. I find that wherever I am, sharing a meal with someone is very human, an aspect only accentuated by strange faces around a table in a strange land.

Some *albergues* ask you to leave your shoes and trekking poles at the door, and some don't. Some have coin-operated washing machines, and some don't. Some will do your laundry for a couple euros. Some have communal dinners and breakfasts. Some have coin-operated massage chairs. Some rent private rooms. The point is that *albergues* come in all shapes and sizes, and there's nothing wrong with checking the alternatives before choosing one, including asking to see the rooms and facilities. That said, much of the Camino is about simplifying your life, if only for a short time. You will get more than your money's worth for eight bucks.

Hotels

Hotels on the Camino range from the very basic to paradors, luxury hotels in converted monasteries, city halls, and other old and grand buildings.

There is nothing wrong with staying in a hotel. When Hape Kerkelring wrote his Camino narrative, some took issue with the fact that he stayed in hotels, but they're just being churlish. Throughout its history, people on the Camino have stayed in whatever accommodations they could afford and chose to stay in. However you walk the Camino is your pilgrim experience.

Most hotels are inexpensive, but many don't have single rooms. If you can find a friend, or brought one with you, a double room is usually 30 euros or less per person. Even if you pay for a double by yourself, it's still cheap compared to a traditional vacation.

Unless you're shelling out the money for it, don't expect more from a hotel than a clean room, a bathroom to yourself, and some privacy. However, after sleeping with 30 or more of your closest friends in an *albergue*, that privacy goes a long way.

Pensions

Pensions are just inexpensive hotels. Some are more akin to a bed and breakfast here in the states. You can even get a room in a private home sometimes.

Camping on the Camino

It's not unheard of, but it's rare. If you do decide to camp out, you'll need a larger pack, a tent, tarp or bivy, a ground cloth, and a sleeping pad and bag. Your local outfitter will be able to help you purchase those items, but you could also skip a few of them for a more Spartan camping experience.

Remember that the area around the Camino may be empty in places, but that doesn't mean it's not owned by someone. You are a stranger in their land, you could be a trespasser too, and that's not a very polite thing to be. Ask permission if you see someone who looks like he owns the place; you might get told no, but you might also get invited to dinner. As with all outdoor activities, leave no trace.

Bedbugs (*chinches*)

Bedbugs do exist on the Camino, but they are rare. These small bugs live in sheets and textiles and leave small, itchy bumps. They are very difficult to get rid of. You can treat your bedding, clothing, and backpack with repellant specifically meant for bedbugs before you go. I don't stress about this issue.

Which accommodation is best?

I stayed at a mix of *albergues* and hotels, typically determined by when I wanted to stop, whether I was with someone else, or if I spotted a friend. While the hotels are more comfortable, the communal experience of the *albergue* is, for me, an important part of the Camino. Certainly they are the best option for your budget.

8. Health and Safety on the Camino

The next two chapters deal with physical preparation for the Camino as well as what medicines to take and what a first aid kit should contain. Before I get to that, here are some of the more common health and safety concerns about the Camino.

The Camino is safe, yet as with any physical undertaking, there are risks. Few pilgrims will encounter life-threatening dangers, but they do happen, and everyone should know about the signs and symptoms, both for their own good and so they can be of service to other pilgrims.

Emergencies

God forbid you should experience an emergency while in Spain or on the Camino, but the risk does exist. Fortunately, wherever you are, including on the Camino, you are unlikely to be alone, and if you are, it won't be for long.

As safe as the Camino is, a few people die on the trail every year, either by being struck by cars or by over-exerting themselves and succumbing to heart failure. Be aware of your surroundings, and be physically and medically prepared. You should talk to your doctor before you go to ensure you are healthy enough for the preparation and the journey.

The emergency number in Spain (and most of Europe) is 112. Here are a few words you may need, but hopefully never will:

- Ambulance = *Ambulancia*
- Police = *Policía*
- Fire = *Bomberos*
- Doctor = *Médico*

Blister treatment

Blisters are probably the most common ailment on the Camino, and there's really no predicting who will get them. If you follow my footwear and sock advice, you'll be less likely to suffer through them. If you do get them, knowing how to treat them is crucial. You should talk to your doctor about how to recognize and treat a blister before you go.

Blisters form because of friction against the skin. They start off as "hotspots" that feel just like they sound, an area on your foot that feels almost like a very minor burn. The friction is damaging the first few layers of skin, and the body responds by filling the area with fluid, pushing those layers of skin out and creating the blister.

First, if you feel a hot spot, stop walking and treat it. The only excuse not to stop immediately is that doing so would be dangerous. Otherwise, stop. You are much less likely to get a blister if your treat the hot spot immediately – it takes very little time or distance for a hot spot to become a blister.

To treat a hot spot, examine it, your shoe, and your sock, and ask yourself if it's as simple as adjusting something to decrease friction. It's probably not that simple. Next, if your socks are damp, change them. Wetness makes friction worse. Then cover the hot spot with something specifically meant to cover a blister, like the products mentioned below.

The unfortunate fact is that the treatment for a hot spot and for a blister is the same: cover it, stay off of it, and wait. On the Camino, of course, you can't stay off it, so all you can do is cover it and hope it doesn't turn into a blister, and if it does turn into a blister, still keep it covered. There's nothing more you can do for a blister than what you should already be doing for a hotspot, with the exception of applying antibiotic ointment to it before covering it.

My preferred blister treatment is Molefoam. It's a thicker version of Moleskin, which is a smooth fabric with a strong adhesive backing. The smoothness of the fabric helps reduce friction, and the strong adhesive keeps the bandage in place and from becoming another source of friction. The thinner Moleskin is especially useful for the small and curvy areas of your foot because it's more flexible, but I prefer the thicker Molefoam. For me, it does a better job dispersing the friction and acts as a cushion. Try both during your practice hikes if need be. I carry one package of Molefoam with me on my hiking trips, and one sheet of Moleskin (three or four sheets come in a package). That knife you brought, or the scissors in your first aid kit, can cut a piece just the right size.

When I do get a blister, I'm always sure to use antibiotic cream on it after showering and whenever I cover it. I check it when I stop during the day to see how it's holding up, I keep it as clean as possible, and I change the cover as needed.

Another treatment is called Compeed. This is a piece of waterproof, thick, flexible plastic with a very powerful adhesive. It works just like Moleskin, but it's meant to stay on until the blister heals, including in the shower. I tried this once without success (it turned into a gooey mess when it got wet), but many people swear by Compeed. Whatever product you buy, read and follow the instructions on the package.

Here's what not to do to a blister: pop or pierce it. Blisters can become infected, and they are more likely to become infected if they are open. Think of your skin as a bacteria-resistant barrier, because that's what it is. The fluid that accumulates in the blister is actually helping you, and it will eventually be reabsorbed by your body.

Sometimes blisters pop themselves, or more likely depending on where it is on your foot, you'll step on it, and it will just pop (and you'll feel it, and it will be kinda gross, but not typically painful). Just keep it clean and covered, apply antibiotic ointment when you cover it, and keep on keeping on.

How do you know if your blister is infected? If the blister or the area around it starts to feel hot to the touch, is discolored, or is abnormally painful, it might be infected. If it does rupture, the fluid that comes out should be clear and odorless; it it's colored or smells bad, it's almost certainly infected. If that happens, find a pharmacy or doctor. The *hospitaleros* at the *albergues* are especially helpful resources in this situation, and pharmacists along the Camino are experienced with blisters.

So to review how to treat a blister:

- Cover the blister with a product specifically meant to cover a blister
- Follow the directions on the blister product you are using
- Use antibiotic cream
- Change the blister cover at least twice a day – once before starting out for the day, once after showering, and anytime the cover wears out or peels off.
- DO NOT POP, PIERCE, OR DRAIN A BLISTER!
- Look out for infection – heat, discoloration, severe pain; milky, opaque, or odiferous drainage – and see a medical professional if you see these signs

Dehydration

Dehydration is probably the second most common ailment on the Camino. Yes, dehydration can prove fatal, but that shouldn't be a major concern on the Camino – water is plentiful. The trick is carrying enough. There are plenty of opportunities to refill, either at fountains or at bars.

There is a saying that says if you are thirsty, it's too late and you're already dehydrated. That is flatly untrue. Is being hungry a sign of starvation? Of course not! Thirst is your body's way of telling you to drink something. It is not a sign that you are already dehydrated, but a sign that you should hydrate.

There is no magic formula for how much water you need to drink. Err on the side of caution and carry more than you believe you'll need (on any trail in any weather, always). You'll get a feel for how much water you need during your practice hikes. I carried three liters during my Camino.

The signs of dehydration include extreme thirst; concentrated (dark) urine; dry skin, lips, and mouth; headache; dizziness; and lightheadedness. The signs of extreme dehydration include a worsening of the above symptoms; rapid pulse and respiration; shriveled, inelastic skin; and confusion. Someone suffering from dehydration should drink water or a sports drink and get out of the sun until symptoms subside. Someone suffering from severe dehydration should seek emergency medical care.

Sunburn, heatstroke, hypothermia

In terms of exposure to the elements, sunburn is the most common threat, but heatstroke and hypothermia are possibilities as well. I strongly suggest reading up on these conditions, their symptoms, and how to prevent them in authoritative medical sources, and perhaps discuss these with your doctor when you see her to talk about whether you are healthy enough for the Camino.

Sunburn is a risk on the Camino as with any outdoor activity. If you are particularly susceptible to sunburn, you should consider wearing long pants and sleeves. Everyone hiking in the warm months, even on a cloudy day, should apply sunscreen and reapply it throughout the day. In the cold months, consider sunscreen because prolonged exposure can result in sunburn even on a cold day.

Heatstroke (hyperthermia, or sometimes called sunstroke) is also a possibility. On hot days with much exertion, getting overheated is possible and potentially dangerous. Anyone walking the Camino in the summer is at risk of heatstroke. Preventing heatstroke requires staying hydrated, trying to avoid sunburn, and keeping the sun off your head. Wear a wide brim hat or a hat with a flap that covers your neck and ears. Rest when needed, preferably in the shade or indoors if the weather is hot. On hot days, rise early and try to complete your day's walk before noon. Heatstroke becomes more likely the more you exert yourself – there's nothing wrong with taking a rest day.

Symptoms of heatstroke include an elevated body temperature, altered mental state, nausea, vomiting, flushed skin, rapid pulse and respiration, and headache.

Anyone experiencing these symptoms should cease exertion and get out of the sun, preferably into an air-conditioned vehicle or building. Anyone exhibiting severe symptoms – body temperature over 103 degrees, altered mental state, no sweating or urination, increased pulse and respiration – should seek emergency medical care immediately.

Hypothermia, a low body temperature, is a possibility in cold weather, even in the fall or spring. It is, however, unlikely for most pilgrims unless they are making their pilgrimage in the winter, but you can get hypothermia any time you are cold, wet, and especially when you are cold and wet, no matter the time of year. Wet clothing, even if it is only wet from sweat, saps heat from your body. During the cold months and at higher elevations, it is important to know the weather before setting out. Ask locals and heed their advice.

The key to preventing hypothermia is to dress in layers and stay dry. Signs of hypothermia include shivering, lips and skin turning blue, dizziness, hunger, nausea, increased pulse and respiration, trouble speaking, confusion, fatigue, and lack of coordination. As hypothermia worsens, shivering ceases, and physical coordination and confusion get worse. People exhibiting signs of hypothermia should get warm and dry as quickly as possible. Those showing severe signs of hypothermia should seek emergency medical care immediately.

Crime on the Camino

Crime does occur on the Camino, but it's rare and usually just involves petty theft. However, in 2015 an American woman went missing on the Camino, and her body was found several months later. It appears that she was murdered. This is a tragedy for her family and a violation of the pilgrim community. I grieve for her. But I will not let the man who did this change what the Camino is and what it means, nor does this terrible incident change the fact that almost 238,000 people completed the Camino in 2014. The Camino is safe, much more so than many American cities.

Locals respect the Camino, and they understand the importance of the Camino to their local economies. I feel safer on the Camino alone than I do walking with friends in some of the neighborhoods in my own city.

Women on the Camino

Many women walk the Camino alone. Or really, they begin the Camino alone. The Camino is not a wilderness trail, and it is not remote – people make friends and walk together, and even if they do not, they are never far from other pilgrims. None of the women I met on the Camino expressed any trepidation, and most of them, like me, were making their pilgrimage solo.

Getting lost

Getting lost is fairly common, but staying lost takes effort. It's easy to miss a way marker, but they are so frequent that it's difficult to go far without realizing that you've missed it. Of course it is easier to get lost in the dark and the fog, and both of these last later into the morning in Spain due to the country being in the Central European Time Zone. Rarely will you have to backtrack too far to find the spot where you lost the trail.

If you really and truly lose the trail, use your judgment and either backtrack or wait for someone to come along. Perhaps your smartphone can tell you where you are. If you are somewhere where there is a risk of falling and you don't have any visibility, <u>stop</u> walking until you can see.

Stray dogs

I hesitate to say this is a myth, because there have been accounts of people encountering stray dogs singly or in packs. Yet no one I met encountered aggressive dogs on the Camino. I encountered several "strays", but I believe they were just left loose to wander until dinnertime, as dogs often are in rural areas. The ones that weren't indifferent toward me were friendly.

If you do encounter an aggressive dog, try shouting at it to scare it away. If that doesn't work, throw a rock or stick. If that doesn't work, back up without turning around and try to go around it.

Traffic

Fatalities do happen on the Camino, most of them the result of traffic accidents. The Camino runs along, over, and across roads and interstates, some remote and others in towns. Parts of the Camino are on the highway itself, with not so much as a guardrail between you and traffic. These places are the exception, and the Camino is being continually adjusted to avoid these spots, but they are present. On these sections, walk on the left side of the road (against traffic) so that you can see oncoming cars, make eye contact with drivers, and react. Take your headphones out when walking on or near roads so you can hear traffic coming, look both ways when crossing a street, and be careful!

Part III

Preparing for the Camino

9. Physically preparing for the Camino.

Walking is hard. If you're like most people, you don't think it is, because you never walk very far, but walking is hard, and walking very far is very hard. You will discover muscles and tendons you didn't think about before, usually because they're causing you pain, and if you thought standing on your feet all day was tough, wait until you walk on them all day long. If you doubt it, consider that walking applies at about 1.5 times your body weight of force to your feet. Those thin layers of skin, fat, muscle, tendon, and bone that are the soles of your feet are supporting your entire body, your pack weight, plus 50%. For a person weighing in at 150 pounds and carrying a 30-pound pack, that's 270 pounds. Now, depending on your stride, one mile could consist of anywhere from 1800 to 2800 steps. For me, a mile is about 2200 steps, which makes a 10-mile day – a modest day – 22,000 steps. Imagine someone hitting the soles of your feet with 270 pounds of force 22,000 times. The first 10,000 probably won't hurt, but it's downhill from there. And quickly.

I probably shouldn't have told you that because the unfortunate fact is that foot pain doesn't really go away. I talked to pilgrims who had been on the Camino for three weeks, and I've talked to long distance hikers who have taken on considerably more challenging hikes than the Camino, and everyone agrees that your feet will hurt. This chapter is more about minimizing all the other discomforts of the Camino. If at the end of the day all that hurts are your feet, you're having a great day!

First, talk to your doctor. Are you healthy enough for the Camino, and for that matter, are you healthy enough to get healthy enough for the Camino? After traffic accidents, most fatalities on the Camino are caused by heart attacks suffered by people who were not physically healthy enough for the rigors of the trail. I'm not a doctor or any kind of health care professional, so please talk to your doctor and take my advice for what it is – lay advice that you follow at your own hazard.

Second, consider your infirmities in general. Are you overweight? Do you have bad knees, hips, ankles, or a bad back? Are you in good shape, or even phenomenal shape? Anything you can do to get in better shape will help you on the Camino, and help you period.

Everyone needs to prepare for the Camino. Walking for 15 miles with something on your back is not a normal activity for anyone other than park rangers. Preparing needn't be burdensome, though. At a minimum, you just need to load up your pack with everything that you're taking with you and start walking as often as you can. However, that's the minimum, and it doesn't necessarily reflect the best situation for everyone.

Let's assume you're in good shape. You're physically fit, and your body is sound. In your case, you need to prepare yourself for the rigors of the Camino, namely making use of the muscles you don't normally make use of, getting used to the weight of a pack, letting the skin on the soles of your feet toughen up. That can be accomplished just by adding some hiking, with a loaded pack, to your routine. Shoot for ten miles a week at a minimum, a decent Saturday hike.

Let's say you're not in good shape. Let's say you are largely inactive. Can you still do the Camino? Yes, but it will be slower and harder, and you're preparation needs to focus on getting your body accustomed to physical stress. Your preparation is about minimizing discomfort down the road - getting your shoulders and neck used to the strain of a pack, getting your ankles and knees and hips used to constant movement, building up muscular endurance in your legs, increasing your lung capacity, strengthening your lower back. All of these areas will be under strain they are not used to.

So here are my recommendations on physically preparing for the Camino:

- Consult your physician
- Start preparing early, and ease your way into your routine. Let your body tell you what it is ready to do. Exercise should be uncomfortable, but never painful

- Develop a well-rounded workout routine. If you do it right, you actually don't have a choice but to develop a well-rounded routine

The importance of balancing your routine cannot be overstressed. Here's a little refresher on how your body works with regards to physical activity and exercise:

- Your muscles need oxygen to work. Oxygen is inhaled through the lungs and stored in your blood, which your heart delivers throughout your body.
- When your muscles are working harder, they need more oxygen
- To provide that oxygen, you start breathing harder to take in more oxygen, and your heart beats faster to deliver that oxygen to your muscles faster
- That system yields an obvious corollary: the more efficient any one of those systems (muscles, heart, lungs) works, the more efficient all the other systems will work, too. Make your muscles work better while demanding less oxygen, and the less your lungs will need to breath faster and the less your heart will need to pump faster. Make your heart stronger, and it will deliver more oxygen to your muscles with less heavy breathing. Make your lungs stronger, and they will take in oxygen more easily.

So yes, you should lift weights and do cardiovascular exercise. I have a weight lifting and cardio routine that works for me regardless of whether I'm preparing for a hike. Design your own routine, or ask for help from your doctor, a personal trainer, or the people who work at your gym.

There is a common misperception that weight lifting results in a lot of added muscle mass, and that's not accurate. You can lift weights and build strength and endurance without building mass. You will be carrying a fairly heavy pack, and you want your neck, shoulders, lower back, hips, thighs, and calves to be used to the weight and to how long you will be carrying it. You can read more about different types of weight lifting, but the short answer is that to build strength and endurance, you need lots of repetitions and weights of medium heaviness. If you're interested, read up on the subject, and if you're not already a weight lifter, I recommend speaking to your doctor and getting in touch with a personal trainer to help you design a workout.

Get out and hike. My training hikes are typically on Sundays so that I have enough time to get in some good miles. It's important to hike with the gear you'll have on the Camino for two reasons. First, you want to test your gear. Things you take for granted may not work: are your socks comfortable? How about your underwear? Would it be helpful to have anything else with you? Is there anything you can get rid of? Are you loading your pack efficiently? Do you know how to best adjust your pack?

Second, you want to be used to carrying all this gear. I actually do my practice hikes with all manner of junk I don't need. Tent, sleeping pad, stove, fuel canister, extra clothes – anything to add weight. With water, my pack typically adds up to 45 pounds, at least 50% more than I take on any trip that doesn't involve sleeping outside. Start out hiking with the gear you are taking, and then for your last few practice hikes, carry the kitchen sink. When you step on to the Camino a week later, it will feel easier, if not easy, by comparison. This is actually common sense. Think of it this way: an Olympic wrestling match is six minutes long, but the athletes prepare for it by practicing 4 hours a day or more.

Hike on varied terrain. My practice hikes in 2013 consisted of the C&O Canal Towpath trail and the Mount Vernon Trail. Both of those are very flat (they run alongside the Potomac outside DC), and are prepared surfaces. I was able to knock out a lot of miles on these, but the flatness suckered me into believing that my pace was much faster than it really is, and it didn't work my leg muscles or heart/lungs the way I needed to.

You want to hike on flat ground and hills. The Camino is of course a mix of both, with some types of terrain lasting for extended stretches. You want to not only prepare yourself for all types of terrain, but observe how your body handles it. How hard are you breathing going uphill? How much do your quads burn? How much do your feet hurt? How fast are you going? This last one is important. I had myself believing that I hiked at about 3 miles an hour, which is respectable for long distance hiking. I found out that on realistic terrain, it was closer to 2.5 and as low as 2 miles an hours by the end of the day. If you know how fast you are, you'll be better able to plan. For the same reason, you want to hike on varied surfaces.

You want to hike at least one very long hike while preparing. You still want to pace yourself and avoid injury, but you need to build up to hiking longer distances. My first training hike was 12 miles, the last 3 of which were agonizing. It was too much for a first hike, but afterwards I was averaging 15-mile days, and they weren't so bad. My longest was an overnight trip that ended up being 36 miles over about 30 hours, and it was agonizing. But my longest day on the Camino ended up being a little over 20 miles, and while it hurt and I was exhausted at the end of it, it wasn't agonizing.

Lastly, part of the point of practice hikes is to reveal your weaknesses at home where you can deal with them rather than on the Camino, where dealing with them will be much more difficult. Are blisters a problem for you? Try different remedies, including different socks, wearing one sock versus two, Moleskin, Molefoam (my favorite), Compeed, Bodyglide or any other remedy you want to try. Problem with a joint? Maybe you can strengthen that joint through a specialized exercise. Talk to a doctor or physical therapist about it. In retrospect, I'm thrilled that I got blisters on my practice hikes. It toughens the skin as they heal, and I figured out how best to prevent and treat blisters for me.

Prepare for the weather. If you're going in the summer, make sure you spend some time outside. It's hard enough hiking in 95-degree weather if you're used to it, so make sure you arrive used to it. (Sorry to anyone who doesn't live where it gets that hot).

Spend some time in the sun. I'm not suggesting that you set out to get a tan, but if you step out onto the Camino officer-worker-pale, you'll end up with sunburn for sure. Use strong sunscreen whenever you spend time outside, and reapply it throughout the day.

Don't let the prospect of rain keep you from a practice hike. It might rain on the Camino, after all. Think of it as a good way to check your rain gear. I recently did nine miles in a state park on a very humid

June day, and I was so happy when it started raining – it cooled everything off, including me, and cut the humidity out of the air. I didn't even bother with a rain jacket.

Don't let the prospect of heat keep you from a practice hike, BUT ADJUST YOUR HIKE. I live in St. Louis, an area that produces as high a heat index as anywhere in the country. I'm not going to make myself miserable, and endanger my health, to get in a practice hike. I will, however, go out early in the day, take more water than I think I'll need, and cut my hike short with the goal of being back before noon. Same goes for hiking in cold conditions (yes, you still need a lot of water when it's cold out).

It's important to take at least one day of rest per week from your workout routine. When you exercise, you are basically damaging tissue, especially in the case of resistance training. You are damaging tissue, and your body rebuilds it stronger than it was before. That's how people build muscle, and note that it's actually not the burning sensation that is damaging the muscle either. It's the act itself – the lactic acid build up is a metabolic byproduct. But your body cannot rebuild itself instantly. It needs time. If you damage the same muscles repeatedly without giving them time to repair, you will never gain any strength. It takes about 48 hours to rebuild muscle, so when you design your routine, you need to give each muscle group 48 hours between exercises to be repaired. Hence the importance of taking a rest day.

If you are in reasonable shape and start preparing for your trip 12 weeks out, you should be ready by the time you hit the Camino. If you need to get in shape, start preparing earlier.

10. Shopping and packing for the Camino

This chapter is really the impetus for this book. The more I learned about hiking by actually doing it, the more I came to look askance at so many books that attempt to tell novice hikers what they needed on the Camino. Some of them got the basics right but lacked detail. Others didn't give advice so much as instructions, which is the author's way of saying that their way is the only right way. Others just gave bad advice. What I'm hoping to do here is to give you options so that you make your own decisions.

Packing for the Camino is not that different from packing for any trip: you'll need a piece of luggage, shoes, clothing, medicine, paperwork, and a few other items. The difference is in the type and functionality of what you need. It's really nothing to be intimidated by.

There is this ridiculous rule of thumb that says a hiker should carry no more than 10% of their body weight. I have a hard time picturing whoever came up with this rule doing an extended overnight trip with no resupply. I don't say that to suggest that you should carry more than 10% of your body weight, but to point out that someone hiking the Pacific Crest Trail (2,663 miles from Mexico to Canada) is hiking on much harder terrain than the Camino, is carrying a good deal more than 10% of their body weight, and is doing it for six months as opposed to the Camino's one, carrying food, tents, sleeping gear, and water treatment for a week or more without resupply. These people are not superheroes - they're just like you and me.

I don't want to downplay the importance of minimizing the amount of weight you carry on the Camino, but I do want to point out that there is a difference between minimizing and obsessing. Some people obsess about their pack weight, and in my opinion, people on the whole cause themselves way too much stress about it. My philosophy for packing for any hike is to decide what I need, then to decide what I *really* need, then to decide if there are lighter weight alternatives or modifications.

On a note of trail etiquette, it's considered rude to discuss the merits of another person's gear with that person, and it's considered by many more to be a boring topic of conversation when on the trail, except when seeking specific advice. Off trail, most people love to talk gear and give advice.

Where to shop

No, this book isn't sponsored by anyone, and I'm not getting paid by any outfitter or retail outlet (but if wishing made it so…). Store and brand recommendations are entirely candid.

Recreational Equipment, Inc. (REI) is the main outdoor equipment retailer in the US. They have a knowledgeable staff and excellent selection. They are also a co-op that you can join for a one-time $20 lifetime membership, and you'll get up to 10% back on eligible purchases (which is almost anything you pay regular price on; you get the money back in the form of a dividend, in credit or cash, in the Spring). That will add up to quite a bit by the time you're done outfitting yourself for the Camino. They also have a no-questions-asked return policy, which is especially advantageous as you're trying out gear on your practice hikes. Don't take advantage of the policy, but use it appropriately as needed. Returned items end up in periodic garage sales at REI stores, and these are good opportunities to get quality gear at low prices.

Campmor is a catalogue outlet based in New Jersey. They carry a large selection and are generally less expensive than other stores by a few dollars. I feel that the discount is a wash compared to REI's co-op member dividend, they don't have as forgiving a return policy, and their only store is in New Jersey, so you can't try anything on unless you happen to live nearby.

Amazon carries everything these days, including packs and boots. You can try things on in a store, then buy them on Amazon, though I don't find that Amazon is much, if at all cheaper, and returns can be a hassle. For the small miscellaneous items you'll need, Amazon is a good bet, though.

Camino-specific items

The first thing you need is a *credencial*. This is the document that proves that you are a pilgrim. Without it, you can't stay at *albergues*. To prove to the cathedral authorities in Santiago that you have earned your *compostela* (the certificate attesting to your accomplishment), you need to get your credencial stamped at least once a day, and after reaching Sarria (111km from Santiago), you'll need to get it stamped at least twice a day. It sounds like a hassle, but it's actually convenient and a joy. You can get it stamped at albergues and bars, and the document becomes a narrative of your journey. Mine is my most prized possession.

You can wait until you get to your starting point to get your credencial, or you can arrange to have one sent to you by your country's cofraternity of Saint James. They're not all the same, so if you go back in the future, get one from a different cofraternity or starting point. In the US, you can request one from AmericanPilgrims.com (and it's nice to leave a donation).

While not necessary, most pilgrims carry a scallop shell on their packs. This is a symbol of the Camino (see Chapter 1), and identifies you as a pilgrim (as if the many items described below don't do that already).

You will need a daily Camino guidebook. The gold standard for English-speaking pilgrims are the ones by John Brierley. His guides list common stage breakdowns, distances, elevation changes, albergues, and towns. You'll use this guidebook to plan your stages, and it contains some interesting prompts for daily meditation. It also contains a brief discussion of items to carry. If you're section hiking, only take the pages with you that you'll need. Bind them in something to keep them together, even just masking tape. I recommend something that will stand up to getting wet since you'll probably carry your guidebook pages on your (sweaty) person.

I strongly recommend a guidebook for Europe and/or Spain (or whatever country you'll be spending most of your time in). Rick Steves' guidebook series *Europe Through the Backdoor* is a best seller for a reason: it's thorough, up to date, and insightful. His books contain information on travel to and from Europe, travel within Europe, money in Europe, traveling with electronics, documents to take, and much, much more. I kept an electronic copy of his Spain guidebook on my smartphone while on the Camino and have stayed in one of his recommended hotels in Santiago (Hotel Suso). His TV series includes an episode on the Camino, and his smartphone app includes two podcasts on the Camino. Rick Steves' travel company also makes money belts (see below) and a cover for binding loose guidebook pages. His website contains a lot of general information about traveling in Europe, and you can purchase a few key travel items directly from his site.

Footwear

There are a couple of old myths about hiking footwear that seem to get repeated from generation to generation. The first is that you need heavy, stiff hiking boots with good ankle "support." The second is that you need to break in your boots thoroughly.

YOU DO NOT NEED HEAVY, STIFF HIKING BOOTS! You are not going mountaineering. You are not carrying heavy loads. Hiking *shoes* are a fine option for the Camino. I've heard of people doing just fine in regular athletic shoes, though I wouldn't advise it because of the rougher areas. Hiking sandals are gaining popularity for warm weather hiking, but bear in mind that sandals don't always fit as well as shoes and that you'll spend more time than you'd like picking pebbles out of your sandals.

This is surprisingly not obvious to a lot of people, but boots that are soft and comfortable don't need to be broken in. Do your gym shoes need to be broken in? The technology overlap between hiking shoes and other kinds of shoes is at the point where most boots don't need more extra care than an everyday shoe. What's more, shoes that fit well generally don't need to be broken in, even stiff leather dress shoes.

So what should you look for in hiking footwear? First, you want a shoe with a good tread. Does it look like it will grip a wet or slick surface, like a gravelly hillside? Vibram soles are now very common on hiking footwear. If you see their name on the shoe, it's a safe bet that they have a good sole.

Second, is the shoe waterproof? Water will get in through the tops and around the edges of the tongue if you submerge your foot, but it's nice being able to walk through a couple inches of water, or even just some wet grass, without getting your feet wet. I only buy boots that have a Gore-Tex lining between the inner and outer layers of the shoe's upper. Gore-Tex is a thin membrane that breathes, allowing moisture to evaporate, but doesn't allow water in. Most shoemakers also have their own version of Gore-Tex that they call by another name, and they work just as well. Sometimes with Gore-Tex if your boot gets very wet, you'll notice that your foot feels wet but actually isn't.

Are they breathable? Most shoes breathe, including leather boots. Some shoes even have mesh side panels. The exception is if they have a waterproof membrane that isn't Gore-Tex or a similar product, or if they've been finished with certain kinds of chemical water proofer or polish. On this last point, go with your gut- does it look like air is going to pass through there? If it's shiny, probably not (and these shoes are going to get messed up - why would you want shiny hiking boots?).

Does the shoe have a rand? The rand is the strip of material that covers the front of the toe. On most boots, it's part of the sole (or at least appears to be) and is made of the same material. This material protects your toes (and you shoes) from all the things you can stub your toes on.

Size AND Width. Your feet swell when you walk. They can swell up to two shoe sizes larger than normal. So when you buy a hiking boot, buy one full size up AND one full width up. I hike in New Balance boots that are 10EEEEEE. Bear in mind that you might be the kind of hiker that prefers two pairs of socks.

A "wide" shoe width corresponds to an EE width in most shoes. Pay attention to the letters, not whether the salesman or website says it's wide.

Keep in mind that a size 9D is not the same across brands, or even across shoes made by the same brand.

When you go to buy your boots, go in the afternoon when your feet will be slightly larger than first thing in the morning. In the store, try on the boots with the socks you'll most likely be wearing. Here's how to try on hiking boots:

1) Lace them up and walk around the store. Does your heel slip? Does the toe box or heel feel tight? Does the arch feel too high or too low? Does the shoe feel too tight or way too loose? Yes - put them back. These shoes will cause you pain and give you blisters. No - proceed to step two.

2) Most stores have a short wooden ramp you can walk down to see if your toes will hit the front of the boot when going downhill (which results in lost toenails after a while). Yes - try a half size larger. No - move to step three.

3) On the carpet, stomp your feet in a forward motion, like you're coming to a very sudden halt. Do your toes hit the front? Yes, and it hurts. Put these back. Yes, but it doesn't hurt. These could be the shoes for you. No - either these are too large or they're laced too tightly. You toes should hit the front if you really stomp, but they shouldn't be smashed into the front. The stomp test is kind of a crapshoot, but it's a good indicator.

These tests aren't foolproof. It's ultimately a judgment call: does this shoe feel like it will be comfortable after 15 miles? The corollary to not needing to break in your modern hiking boots is that modern hiking boots don't break in. If it's not comfortable in the store, it will NEVER be comfortable on the trail. And never let a salesman tell you otherwise. If they do, they don't know what they're talking about and/or just want to make a sale, and your feet are your best friends and worst enemies on the Camino. Treat them kindly.

Backpacks

Everyone has bought shoes before: the product if not the particulars are familiar. Not so with backpacks. A sporting goods store could carry dozens of different backpacks, and this choice is just as consequential as buying boots.

These backpacks are not what you took your stuff to school in. They are heavier, they are adjustable in a bunch of different ways, and they come in sizes. So when you go to the store, ask to be fitted for a backpack. The process is simple. They have a plastic sheet with some markings on it (they're inches) and a nylon belt. Put the belt around your waist with the plastic sheet in the back. The salesman will check to make sure that the middle of the belt is situated on your Iliac Crest (the tops of your hip bones), which is where the middle of your pack's waistbelt should sit, and then he'll press the sheet to where your neck, shoulders, and back meet (typically where most people have a small convex curve of the spine). Taking note of the marking, he'll tell you whether you're a small, medium, or large. Then you unbuckle the sheet from your waist and stop feeling ridiculous.

Some packs don't come in small, medium, or large, though. They come in small/medium or medium/large instead. The salesperson can tell you which to get.

What if you're on the rotund side? Sometimes the length of the pack for you will be a medium, but the medium comes with a smaller belt size than will fit you. Then get the large. A larger size may ride a bit high on your shoulders, but the belt is the load-bearing part of the pack - you can't skip it.

Backpacks typically have frames. It used to be that every pack was made on an external (you could see it) aluminum frame. Now most packs have an internal fame (it's built into the backpack), and it's made of aluminum or carbon fiber. There are also frameless packs, which save some weight, but I personally think they're less comfortable because the purpose of the frame, in addition to providing a structure to the pack, is to take weight off of your shoulders. The weight of the pack is held by the frame, the frame is held up by the belt, the belt is around your hips – your center of gravity and strength. Carbon fiber weighs less than aluminum but costs more.

Backpacks have a ton of pockets. A pack should have 5 to 7 pockets, including the main compartment, but that's not to say that one with more or fewer is a bad pack. The main compartment is just that - it holds most of your junk.

The top of the pack is a pocket. It's a handy place to keep things you want easily accessible like keys, important papers, a little spare cash, your pocket knife, your lunch, etc. Sometimes these are detachable and form a fanny pack - a nice feature I've never had occasion to use.

There should be a pocket on either side above the hipbelt. These fit a water bottle, but note that even if you can get a bottle out of one of those pockets with the pack still on your back, you probably won't be able to get it back in without taking your pack off.

There should be an outside pocket, called a shovel pocket, which covers the main compartment and usually has no zipper but does have a buckle. It's handy for storing things you want easily accessible. A rain jacket, or some TP (or if you're camping, a trowel for digging catholes).

On either wing of your hip belt should be a zippered pocket. They're not large but hold things you might want quickly. I keep a cell phone in them, sometimes a protein bar, sometimes a pocketknife, and usually a washcloth for mopping my brow and cleaning my hands.

Your pack might also have a separate compartment for your sleeping bag. This is especially common on larger packs, and while nice for organization and accessibility, it is not necessary. I've yet to come across a pack that did not have a zipper at the bottom so that separate compartment or not, it's easy to get your sleeping bag out without having to disturb everything else in your pack.

A nice feature on one of my packs is a map pocket on the underside of the top pocket. It's a convenient place to keep not just maps but your important papers, especially on an international trip.

Others features you should look for are hydration sleeves and ventilation. Hydration sleeves are dedicated spaces to slip a hydration bladder (see below). On some packs, this sleeve is on the outside of the pack, between the main compartment and the back panel (the part of the packs that rests on your back). On others, this sleeve is inside the main compartment and is really just a nylon pouch for separating the bladder from your stuff, with a small hole in the side of the pack to feed the drinking tube through. I strongly prefer the former setup as a full hydration bladder is a large and unwieldy thing – it's a pain trying to stuff one inside your backpack when it's full of your other stuff. Also, if the bladder does leak, I don't trust the internal nylon sleeves to keep my stuff dry.

Ventilation refers to the way the back panel of the pack is built. There are three kinds. The first type is a standard back panel and doesn't have a special name: it just sits directly on your back, and is often the same material as the loop of Velcro (because the straps are the hook side, to make them adjustable). I strongly advise against this type. It doesn't qualify as ventilation because by sitting directly on the back and being made of a material that doesn't breath, it doesn't ventilate anything. The only advantage to packs with this type of ventilation is that they are usually less expensive.

The second type of ventilation is a mesh back panel. This is sewn to the pack and is made of mesh with some foam in key spots underneath to aid support. Your back closes off most of the airflow, but your back is not pressed directly against the bag, so some air is moving.

The third type of ventilation is the suspended mesh back panel. On this type of backpack, the frame is more curved (while still molding to the shape of your back) to create space between the back panel and the bag itself. Mesh is stretched over the frame, so air is moving between your back and the backpack.

Here's a front and profile view of a pack with a standard back panel:

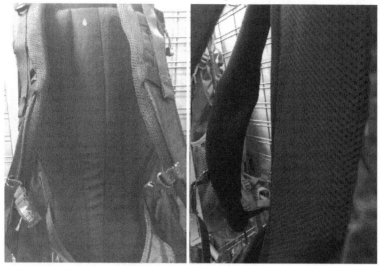

A pack with a standard back panel. Even with the groove down the middle, the wearer's back makes almost complete contact with the back panel, eliminating airflow.

Here's a front and profile view of a pack with a mesh back panel:

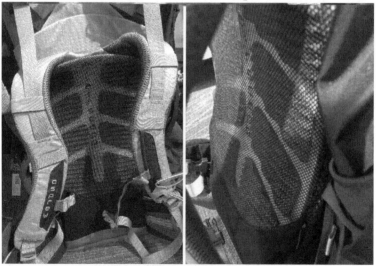

A pack with a mesh back panel. Note that the padding under the mesh is spaced to promote airflow, but that there is still a lot of contact between the back panel and wearer. This pack also features an external hydration sleeve.

Here's a front and profile view of a pack with a suspended mesh back panel:

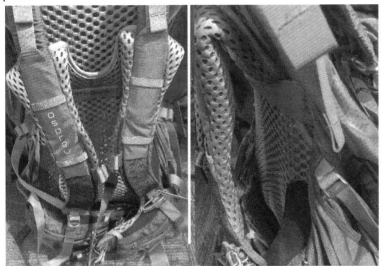

A pack with a suspended mesh back panel. Note the curve of the frame and the two or so inches of space between the back panel and the bag itself.

The suspended mesh back panel gives a lot of airflow, but there is a tradeoff: I have yet to find a backpack with both an external hydration sleeve and a suspended mesh back panel. I suspect this is because the hydration bladder would bulge into the space between the mesh and the bag, canceling out any airflow. I prefer the non-suspended mesh back panel with the external hydration sleeve. I enjoy the airflow of a suspended panel, but realistically, every part of you, including your back, is going to sweat when you hike no matter how much airflow there is. For me, the convenience of the external sleeve cancels out the slight increase in comfort of a suspended panel.

How big of a bag do you need? Someone people say you should buy everything you're going to take with you and then decide how big a bag you need. I say that this approach leads you to taking more stuff than you need. Buying the pack first puts a hard limit on how much stuff you can take: only what fits in the bag. For the Camino, I bought an Osprey Talon 44. The "44" is the volume of the bag in liters. Sometimes you'll see pack volumes in cubic inches, which is actually kind of a pain (2200 cubic inches versus 2600 - how is anyone supposed to intuitively know how much bigger that is?). I think that's the perfect size for the Camino, but not necessarily the perfect pack.

Packs themselves weigh a few pounds, anywhere from one pound for a small bag to six pounds for a large one. The more features, the heavier the bag. Packs in the ultralite class have fewer features and weigh less. You don't need many features, right? And the less weight the better, right? Maybe. The component of a pack that's easiest to save weight on is the padding in the shoulder straps and hip belt. Because padding helps to distribute the weight of the pack, having less padding means that the straps will put more pressure on your shoulders and hips. This means that the amount of padding determines how much weight a pack can hold *comfortably*. My Talon 44 is meant to hold 25 to 40 pounds, but beyond about 30 it's not very comfortable. I have a larger pack, an Osprey Aether 70, that's meant to hold 50 to 65 pounds. The Talon weights 2 pounds, 6 ounces. The Aether weighs 5 pounds, 3 ounces. I prefer the Aether for most hikes - it weighs more, but I don't feel the weight as much because the pack is doing more of the work by distributing the weight better. If only they made the Aether in a smaller size... (hint, hint, good people at Osprey).

When you go to buy your pack, try it on in the store, and ask the salesman to put some sandbags in it so you can feel the weight. Be suspicious: every pack feels fine with 25 pounds in it when you just put it on. Will it really still feel good after 15 miles? You can put some sandbags in a backpack and then go do the rest of your shopping in the store to get a sense of how the pack feels after a half hour, but you still need to make a judgment about how it will feel after six or eight hours of hiking.

Backpacks are adjustable in several ways to provide a close fit that puts the weight of the pack in the right places. Before you put on a backpack, loosen the straps on the hip belt, the shoulder straps, the sternum strap, and the load lifter straps. With your pack on your back, start by buckling the hipbelt and tightening it so that it hugs, but doesn't compress, your hips. Then tighten the shoulder straps as much as you comfortably can; it helps to shrug your shoulders while bending forward to lift the pack up, then tighten the straps by pulling down and back quickly before the pack settles back. Buckle the sternum strap; the purpose of the sternum strap is to keep the shoulder straps from sliding off as you walk; it doesn't need to be tight, and it should go across your sternum, not across your nipples. Lastly, snug down the load lifter straps, which pull the top of the pack closer to the tops of your shoulders so that the top of the pack doesn't sway from side to side or pull backward as you hike. As a last step, you can very slightly loosen your shoulder straps so that the weight of the pack comes to rest more on the hipbelt.

Most packs these days have adjustable torsos. It varies by pack, but the shoulder harness on adjustable packs is often secured to the back panel with Velcro, and in this way the torso length of the pack can be made longer and shorter (within a range, of course – this is not a substitute for the right pack size). If your shoulder straps are not resting on you're your shoulders, your pack is too long for you, and you need to shorten the length if it's adjustable, or return the pack for a smaller one. If all the weight is resting on your shoulders, then the torso length is too short for you. You'll most likely have to try the pack on several times and adjust the torso to the right position for you, but your salesperson can be a great help in making the first adjustments in the store. I like to adjust mine so that the very top of the back panel rests at the very top of my scapulae.

There is also an art to packing a backpack. The goal is to distribute the weight in such a way that the pack and your core – not your shoulders – are doing the work. It's all about putting stuff in the right place, and it's easy. The sleeping bag goes at the bottom. To provide some additional structure to my bag, I like to put my sandals, vertically with the soles facing out, at the bottom on either side of the sleeping bag. The heaviest items in the pack should go in the middle of your back. The Camino doesn't require anything very heavy, so it's a good place to put your second set of clothes or your cold weather gear (if you have any). Above that, you can stash your toiletries and towel. They're the first things you're going to want when you get to an albergue. I keep my rain cover and rain jacket in the shovel pocket, which makes them easy to grab in a hurry. The top pocket contains things I need regularly or might need in a hurry and thus don't want to have to root around in the main compartment of the bag for: first aid kit, lunch, cellphone. The hipbelt pockets can serve a similar role as the top pocket. Lastly, if I have anything I just don't need on the trail itself (like electronics for the plane ride), I stuff it all the way at the bottom, out of my way.

You can find many online videos showing how to fit, adjust, and pack a backpack, including several very good ones on the REI website. Most pack manufacturers also have instructional videos on their websites.

Socks

Socks matter just as much as boots. Every hiker has their own preferred sock strategy. Here are your basic options:
- One thin sock. Keeps your feet cool and feels more natural.
- One thick sock. Adds some cushioning.
- One thin sock (typically a liner sock) under one thick sock. More cushioning, and the liner sock wicks moisture away from your foot and into the thick outer sock. Some also find that the inner and outer socks slide over one another so that the friction is between them and not between your foot and the sock.

The bottom line is all three strategies are meant to prevent blisters, and the only way to figure out which one works for you is trial and error. And like everything else, hiking socks are not like regular socks.

Hiking socks are expensive. There's no getting around it. Figure on spending around $10 per pair, and on discarding some that don't work for you. It's a bummer, but socks are one of those places where you just can't skimp on hiking gear.

Never wear cotton socks while hiking. They absorb moisture rather than wick it away, and that means blisters. And while they seem soft at home, they lose their softness when air-dried (and they take longer to air dry). No, you want wool socks or socks in a technical fabric.

Wool is a great insulator. It wicks moisture. It's soft. And regardless of what you might remember from childhood Christmas sweaters, it doesn't itch. Some, if not most, wool hiking socks are even the very soft Merino wool. Wool socks come in a variety of thicknesses, but most of them are thicker than technical fabrics.

Technical fabrics are designed to have a lot of the same properties as wool. Most liner socks are technical: polypropylene and polyester, mostly (though some come in silk). Technical fabrics do retain odor more than natural fibers, but who's ever heard of a rosy smelling sock anyway? Besides, you'll wash your clothes daily.

SmartWool is a company that makes performance clothing, including socks. Their socks are a treated Merino wool. If you're going with a wool sock, I recommend this brand or a similar technology (other manufacturers treat their Merino socks, too, and use a different trademark name).

My socks are my secret weapon. When I first started hiking, I tried the two-sock method, a polypropylene liner sock under a SmartWool sock. I got blisters. I tried changing my socks mid-day, and I still got blisters. I tried just one sock, and I got blisters. They were concentrated on the balls of my feet where my toes start. I came to the conclusion that the friction from the sock, and not from the boot or ground, was causing my blisters.

I have a thick foot, and it forms a gap between the sole and the toes where my socks can work their way in and move around, causing friction and blisters. I looked into some goofy remedies before finding Injinji socks - these are socks made for runners, and they have individual toes. They're made from treated Merino wool (called NuWool), and they are skin-tight. By being skin tight, they fill in the space between my toes and soles without moving around, causing no friction and no more blisters on the balls of my feet. The only drawbacks are that they're too thin to provide cushioning (though they do come in different thicknesses, all of them thin relative to traditional hiking socks), they wear out quickly, and they take some practice to put on. But they are my favorite piece of hiking gear (and they lead to fun conversations when people see my individually socked toes).

Bottom line is socks are trial and error. Your practice hikes will be key in helping you select the right sock for you. Avoid cotton socks, and find the right fabric, thickness and number of socks for you.

Water

Water is plentiful along the Camino. The water in Western Europe is perfectly potable for Americans – you will not become ill from the tap water. You can even drink from public fountains (the spigot, not the pool) so long as it doesn't have a sign saying you can't, and you can buy bottled water anywhere you stop for about a euro or two. The bottles you buy are just like the reusable bottles in the US, so you can refill them and reuse them.

That's not what I do. I drink a lot of water, two to four liters a day even when I'm not hiking, so I like carrying my water, and I like it to be accessible. The side pockets on your pack will fit a 1-liter Nalgene bottle (Nalgene is a brand name, but it's become synonymous with all plastic water bottles of that size and shape). If you're going to carry nothing else, carry a 1-Liter Nalgene bottle.

But as I said earlier, the side pockets are not accessible when your pack is on your back. Assuming you can twist your arm backward to reach the bottle and get it out, you won't be able to get it back in without taking your pack off. And one liter is not as much water as you think it is. What if, like me, you need to carry three liters? Then you'd need three bottles and three places to put them.

That's where hydration bladders come in. A hydration bladder is a durable plastic bag for holding water with a long, flexible rubber tube for drinking out of. At the end of the tube is a bite valve - when you bite down on it (gently) and suck, water comes out; when you're not biting down on it, it's sealed and doesn't leak. Camelbak is the big brand in hydration bladders, but I actually don't care for their product.

Camelbaks are the original, and they work fine. But the bladder is just a plastic bag with a tube. If you followed my advice, you bought a pack with a hydration sleeve specifically meant to hold a hydration bladder, but your pack is full and bulging into the sleeve. How easy do you think it is to shove a plastic bag full of water into a narrow space that's being impinged upon by the stuff in your pack, keeping in mind that the bladder needs to maintain its shape so the flow isn't blocked? It's a royal pain, especially at 6am when you're trying to walk out the door.

Enter Osprey, the same company that makes all the packs I own. They make a hydration bladder that has two wonderful additions: a stiff plastic backing, and a handle. These give structure to the bladder and make it easy to get it in and out of your hydration sleeve. For my money, I think their bite valve, which also rotates to lock off the flow, is better than Nalgene's, too. These features add a touch more weight, but they save a lot of hassle. Another nice feature is that the Osprey bladders have a loop at the top, and their packs have a small buckle in the hydration sleeve – buckle the bladder in, and it won't slide down to the bottom of your hydration sleeve, taking the tube with it, as you walk.

On any hydration bladder, the drinking tube (not the urethra, I've been assured) just comes out the top, loops down one of the shoulder straps, and secures under some elastic bands on the strap. Water when you want it without having to take off your pack or stop walking, and the weight of the water - the heaviest single item you will carry - is positioned in the middle of the back, where your heaviest items should be, rather than on your sides.

I carry a 2- or 3-liter Osprey bladder as well as a Nalgene bottle on the trail. When I stop, I drink out of the bottle to avoid draining the bladder.

No one likes a bladder infection, in this case mildew or mold. It's absolutely true that a hydration bladder is more difficult to fill (marginally) and to clean (definitely) than a bottle. A Nalgene bottle can be put in the dishwasher, a hydration bladder cannot. You probably won't clean your hydration bladder while on the Camino beyond just a rinse, and that's sufficient. When you're home, though, and between practice hikes, you need to clean it - damp and dark breeds mold, even though hydration bladders contain anti-mold materials. You can buy kits and special tablets to clean hydration bladders. I recommend the kits – they come with a brush that lets you get inside the bladder; a longer flexible brush, like a pipe cleaner, to get into the tube; and a special hanger that holds the bladder open to dry. Just follow the instructions and let the bladder hang long enough to dry out. You may need to hang it upside down from a clothes hanger to make sure it drains completely. Bottom line is just don't put it away wet.

Trekking poles

Almost every pilgrim has a walking stick or trekking poles. I appreciate the emotional pull of a gnarled walking stick – the wood just feels authentic, like something a medieval pilgrim carried. And with some extra hassle, you can mail them back to your home as a souvenir that will mean more and last longer than anything else you might buy along the way. That said, I don't recommend them. Not because they don't do a decent job but because modern trekking poles do a better job.

Trekking poles come in pairs. They're made of aluminum (less expensive) or carbon fiber (lighter weight). The handles are neoprene or cork. They have a metal or rubber tip (usually interchangeable: use the rubber ones for less clacking noise and less scratching up the rocks on the trail – leave no trace). They are adjustable to fit your height. You can also get a modern trekking staff, just like the wooden ones but lightweight and adjustable.

Why use a staff or trekking poles? For safety and support. Poles transfer some of your weight from your legs, and especially knees, to your upper body while allowing you to keep at least two points of contact with the ground at all times. Is there a thigh-high rock in front of you? Plant your poles up there first and pull yourself up. Are you on a steep downhill? Use the polls to slow yourself down. Is the ground uneven or slippery? Having more points of contact makes it less likely you'll fall.

My poles are Black Diamond Ultra Distance poles. They are collapsible to a smaller size and are lighter than most poles, but they're not adjustable and so come in sizes according to height ranges. And yes, you do develop an emotional connection to your trekking poles just like you do a walking stick.

I've seen a lot of hikers incorrectly using their trekking poles. All poles have a wrist strap. Your hand comes in from underneath so that the strap goes across your palm. This transfers your weight to the pole via the strap so that you don't have to white-knuckle the pole to transfer your weight. Sometimes it helps to palm the poles, putting your hands on top of the handles to place more weight on them. This is especially helpful going downhill.

You can't carry trekking poles, staffs, or walking sticks on an airplane. They have to go in checked baggage.

Sleeping bags

This item comes in low on my gear priority list, but I'll give it a thorough overview anyway.

Sleeping bags come in temperature ratings. These ratings are the temperature that the average man or woman could sleep comfortably assuming they are wearing a base layer (long underwear) and a hat. This rating is actually ten degrees colder for men than for women – European Union regulations require the rating to account for the fact that men don't get as cold. Some people say that this rating is actually a survival rating and the manufacturers are pulling a fast one, but for Camino purposes, it's a moot point: you're sleeping inside. Albergue dormitories have a lot of bodies in them, boosting the temperature; they don't always have a lot of windows, and you might not always be near one (and the person who is may want it closed); rural Spain is often not air conditioned; and you're probably going during a warm month. You don't need a sleeping bag rated for sub-freezing temperatures, and you don't want one. The warmer the bag, the heavier and bigger it is.

Sleeping bags are insulated with down (yep, goose feathers, or more likely duck feathers, which are cheaper) or synthetic materials. They're both warm, but the down is warmer for the weight and bulk. In fact, down is the best insulator known to man. We have been unable to discover a material superior to what nature has given waterfowl. The downside to down is that when wet, it loses those insulating properties until it dries, which takes a long time. But again, it doesn't matter because you're sleeping inside. Synthetic down is less expensive, almost as light, and almost as warm. I own two sleeping bags, and both are synthetic, a decision I made to save money. If I were camping in sub-freezing temperatures, then I'd pay for real down.

At home, store your sleeping bag on a hanger or in a large stuff sack, never a compression sack. This prevents the insulation from losing its loft.

For my first Camino, I bought a synthetic sleeping bag with a high temperature rating, 55 degrees. I figured that would be fine, but it was actually a lot more than I needed. For all the reasons I already mentioned, it's warm in *albergues* to the point where I had trouble sleeping. Also, the *albergues* provided a heavy blanket plus a sheet in every place I stayed in. I don't know how often they got washed, but the sheets look liked they got washed daily (they were white, at least). The sleeping bag just became an extra 2 pounds in my pack.

A nice alternative is a sleeping bag liner. This is basically a sleeping bag the same thickness as a sheet and not insulated at all. It provides some warmth, you know it's clean (or at least it's your own filth), and it weighs less and takes up less space than a sleeping bag. They come in silk as well as synthetics; the former is more expensive, but takes up less room and weighs less, while the latter is less expensive and is often treated to repel insects. I don't know if that includes bedbugs, but I figure it can't hurt. Mine is synthetic.

Some people are content to just take a regular bed sheet from their home, and some take a silk sheet to save on weight and space. Ultimately, whether you take a sleeping bag, sleeping bag liner, or sheet depends on personal preference and time of year. When I go on pilgrimage now, I take a liner if it's a warm month and a light sleeping bag if it's a cooler month.

Clothing

Don't wear blue jeans. Yeah, some of the characters in *The Way* are wearing blue jeans. Don't wear blue jeans. In fact, don't wear cotton. Cotton is heavy, it absorbs moisture rather than wicking it away, and it takes a long time to dry. You'll be hand washing your clothes most nights. You don't have the time to let your jeans or favorite t-shirt dry. Besides, on the trail you will be more comfortable in technical fabrics.

Underwear is one of those things that you don't spend too much time thinking about. You pick a style, and you stick with it. And then you think nothing of it going on your first practice hike – until you're halfway into it and your thighs are licorice red and so raw that your own sweat burns. Yeah, that happened to me (more than once). Again, you want underwear in a technical fabric that pulls moisture away, dries quickly, and fits tightly. I recommend boxer briefs, a style I only wear while hiking. They protect my thighs (and other bits too – yeah, that happened, more than once) from one another, and they dry quickly after going up on the wash line. I like the Terramar brand. ExOfficio makes some good ones too. The brand matters less than the style and fabric (quick-dry polyester), though.

The most common pants you'll see on the Camino are convertible hiking pants in polyester. The lower legs zip off to form shorts. They're lightweight, they dry quickly, and they have cargo pockets if you need an extra place to hold something. The big brands here are Columbia and Patagonia, though REI makes good ones too.

Many hiking pants come with a simple nylon belt with a plastic crimp buckle. If not, you can buy one cheaply. The adjustability of these belts is superior to leather and linen, both of which become difficult to adjust when wet or sweaty. It's not uncommon for a belt to loosen up as you walk, and the ability to snug it down just a little bit is ideal.

There are a variety of good-looking outdoor shirts these days, but for actual hiking, I like a t-shirt in a technical fabric. Russell Athletic makes shirts in a material called Dri-Power (other brands have other names for this technology). It breaths well, it dries fast. They're the same shirts I wear to the gym; I own a half dozen.

In the evenings, it can feel pretty good to change into something different from what you wore all day. There are a number of brands that carry outdoor shirts that are a little nicer than a t-shirt but are still lightweight and made of quick-dry material. Columbia is the best known company for these, and I like to change into one of their shirts after hiking all day.

Virtually all hiking clothing, in a technical fabric, is now made with sun protection in mind. There is typically an SPF rating prominently displayed on the tag. Still, use sunscreen, even if it's a cloudy day, and reapply often.

I don't wear bright colors. I'm an earth tones kind of guy. But not when I'm hiking. I wear bright shirts, my shoelaces have hunter orange in them, and my packs are silver, blue, or red. If I get hurt, if I'm ill, if I'm lost, or if I'm just walking near traffic, people will be able to see me. Save the camouflage and earth tones for hunting trips. Hiking pants and shorts tend to come in shades of green and brown, though, so no help there.

You do need a hat of some sort. I don't particularly care for hats (though I look smashing in my trilby), but they do make a huge difference helping you stay cool and feeling good on a hot day. If you're hiking on the Meseta, the guidebooks universally agree that you need a hat to keep the sun off your head and neck and out of your eyes. You can go with a wide brimmed hat, but you can also get a ballcap-style hat that has fabric that covers the back of your neck and your ears. Hats also come in breathable, lightweight fabrics that are designed to help you avoid sunburn, but this is the only area where I don't see anything wrong with cotton. Some people like straw hats because they are light and shed water. Whatever it is, it just needs to be lightweight and functional. I like the ballcap style because you can wear it under the hood of a rain jacket to keep the hood from sagging low over your eyes.

Sunglasses are also a must. Your eye needs to be protected from sun damage as well, and you'll look cool in them. Sunglasses made for athletics often have lenses that cover more of your eye, offering more protection above and to the sides.

Rain gear

This is one of those places where you definitely get what you pay for. You can go cheap and get a plastic or rubber jacket for under $20, but after wearing it for about 5 minutes, you'll regret it deeply. The whole point of a rain jacket is to avoid getting wet, but by choosing a cheap, non-breathable rain jacket, all the moisture (i.e. evaporating sweat) from your body stays inside the jacket. You'll end up soaked in your own sweat (and no one will want to sit by you).

Again, breathable fabrics, and usually this means Gore-Tex for a rain jacket. There are so many options here, but this is pretty straightforward. Look for a jacket that is lightweight, has a hood with a drawstring, and packs down to a small size. Some of them even pack into their own pockets. This is an item I keep in the shovel pocket of my pack, so it's handy.

Two rain jacket tips: buy a larger size than you normally wear, and try it on in the store. You may need to put the jacket on over more than one layer, for instance if it's cold and raining, so the larger size keeps you from hiking through Spain looking like an overstuffed chorizo. The larger size also promotes airflow. Trying it on in the store is also a chance to cinch down the hood to see how it fits; I've found that on some jackets, my field of vision is too small when the hood is cinched, and I've always been very big on seeing where I'm going. A handy trick for this is to wear a ballcap under your hood, though, and you can cinch it down without it impeding your vision.

You'll need a rain cover for your pack. Yes, your pack is probably made out of nylon, and nylon is water resistant, but nylon is not waterproof, and neither are zippers. Some packs, especially smaller ones, have a built in rain cover that's stored in a pouch at the bottom of the pack. These are handy, and I don't understand why every pack doesn't have one. If your pack doesn't have one, you'll need to buy one. They come in sizes and have an elastic cord so you can fit it to your pack well, both to keep it watertight and to keep it from flapping around in the wind. These can also be balled up pretty small and kept in your shovel pocket.

Rain pants are an option I don't take advantage of except in cold weather. I'm just not that concerned about rain. I feel like my jacket is enough for me, and I find the extra layer of pants to be uncomfortable for hiking. But if you don't like being wet, or don't like the idea of hiking in wet pants, or tend to get cold easily, rain pants are handy to have. If you are hiking in potentially cold weather, then rain pants are a must. All the rules about rain jackets hold here too.

If you really want to stay 100% dry (or at least close to it), you can get rain gaiters, too. Gaiters are waterproof sleeves that go over the top of your boot and around your lower leg so that water cannot get in from the top of the boot or tongue.

Should you consider a poncho? Ponchos are cheaper than rain jackets. They're open on the bottom, so by definition they are breathable. They keep most of your legs dry without rain pants. And they are big enough to cover you and your pack. The downside? It's hard to use trekking poles with a poncho on, you lose a lot of range of movement for your arms, they're heavier, and while breathable, they can still trap some moisture around your upper body. Some people prefer ponchos, others don't. It's purely a preference, though it can be a good budget saver, too.

Sandals

You most likely do not want to wear your hiking footwear all day, which works out great because many albergues won't let you wear your muddy, smelly boots inside. Sandals are a good "camp" shoe because they're lighter than shoes and can offer relief from blisters and sore feet. At the end of the day, it's nice to just let your feet breath. You can take a pair that's waterproof for use as shower shoes, but I took my chances with a pair of Teva sandals (the sole is waterproof, the straps are not). Some people prefer Crocs: they are super-light, waterproof, and while unfashionable, they are functional.

Cold weather gear

Whether you need it or not depends on the time of year and your preferences. You know what you need to be comfortable, so just check the average temperatures when you'll be going and decide. If you do need it, here's my advice.

Fleece! It's warm and lightweight, and it breathes. Breathability is especially important in cold weather clothing because however cold it is, you're still exerting yourself, and you'll still sweat. You want that moisture to evaporate. Fleece's drawback is that's it's not windproof, but windproof materials aren't always breathable. If your cold weather gear isn't breathable, you'll end up wet and even colder. So for an outer top layer, consider a fleece jacket or vest. It doesn't need to be thick: 100- or 200-weight fleece will do because...

Layers! Layering traps air between the layers, and your body warms that air, creating natural insulation. If you find that you're still cold despite your fleece jacket, put your rain jacket on over it.

Long underwear is a choice, and it can be a good one if you run especially cold. It comes in all manner of material, but unless you are going in the deep of winter, you want polyester, polypropylene, or silk. Silk is warmer than you'd think, transfers moisture, is extremely light, and packs small, but it's not cheap and doesn't have a long shelf life (even, or perhaps especially, the artificial varieties). Polypropylene is thicker than silk, often coming in a double layer, and is fuzzy-warm. Polyester comes in too many iterations to list here.

Gloves and a hat. A wool knit cap does just fine, as does fleece, but if you're going with fleece, look for a hat with an internal ear band that's windproof. As for gloves, I like mine on the thin side, and if need be I can always jam my hands in my pockets. When you're hiking, your body sends extra blood to your legs muscles. When it's cold, your body sends extra blood to your core. In other words, your hands will get cold if it's chilly out.

An alternative to fleece is down. Down jackets are without doubt the warmest you can buy, and they pack down to a small size. If you're doing your Camino in the winter months, down may be the best choice for you, provided the shell of the jacket is breathable. Down is very warm, however, so consider if you will be too warm with a down jacket or vest given what time of year you're going.

I'm a cautious soul who likes it on the cold side. That's part of why I chose late September for my Camino. Particularly in the mountains, and especially in Galicia, the weather can be cold and damp. It happened to be unseasonably warm weather for that part of the year, so I didn't need the cold weather gear I brought, but I'd take it again. I took a set of long underwear in artificial silk, a thin pair of gloves, and a fleece hat. Just in case.

How many sets of clothes do you need?

Two. One to hike in, and one to not hike in. You'll be able to wash your clothes daily, and because you bought quick-drying technical fabrics, they'll be dry before you go to bed every night (and you should bring them in before dark, especially in Galicia where it gets foggy and damp many evenings). I hike in a pair of convertible pants and a t-shirt, and I spend the evenings in a second pair of convertible pants and a Columbia shirt. For sleeping, I wear a pair of gym shorts

Toiletries

This isn't camping, so you can, and are expected to, bathe and wash your clothes daily. You're sharing close quarters with strangers; it's only courteous that you don't stink. Whatever toiletries you use at home, bring them along. However, don't bring more than a 10-day supply. People in Europe bathe too (despite stereotypes), so you can restock in drug stores along the Camino. You may not get exactly what you like to use, but you'll avoid carrying a lot of heavy toiletries that take up a lot of space. Besides, it's only for a little while.

By now everyone knows that there are limits for carrying liquids and gels onto planes: you can't have any containers that are larger than 3.4 fluid ounces, and they have to all fit in a single, quart-sized Ziploc baggie. Because I'm a frequent business traveler, I actually found out through trial and error that Nalgene makes the best set of travel-sized containers for storing smaller amounts of toiletries. They're durable, and most importantly, the lids stay on and stay tight. They sell sets that include containers of various sizes, including a squeeze bottle. The small-sized set has the perfect sizes for air travel.

Of course the restrictions on the size and number of liquids and gels you can bring onto planes do not apply if you're checking your luggage, but the travel-sized containers are perfect for taking small amounts for hiking: carry only what you need. Use the containers to take the shampoo and conditioner you need, and I also use mine to hold my medications. But when overseas I bring my prescription medications in the original bottles in case I need to show them to a pharmacist.

If you need a prescription medication that is in liquid, gel, or lotion form, you can pack it in your carry-on luggage in its original bottle. Bring a copy of the original prescription. Contact TSA or your airline for details.

One thing to not bring is a bar of soap. A wet bar of soap that doesn't dry out, for instance if it's in a Ziploc bag, turns into goo. Instead, I take some liquid body soap, also in one of my Nalgene containers.

I wear a beard, so when on the Camino I just stop shaving entirely and go *au natural*. If that's not an option for you, carry a disposable razor and the smallest container of shaving cream or lotion you can. I still use a shaving lotion, but if I did decide to shave while hiking, I'd probably choose shaving foam because the travel-sized cans are so small and light.

I suppose it goes without saying that a travel-sized toothpaste, toothbrush, and a small comb are what you need. You can also use a travel-sized deodorant, or just a mostly empty regular size.

You will need your own towel. Regular towels are not ideal for the same reason that regular clothes are not ideal: they are too heavy, too big, and take too long to dry. Instead, pick up a hiking towel from your outfitter. These have a microfiber-like texture, are light, small, and dry very quickly. They come in different sizes up to five feet long. I carry two: one large one for bathing, and a smaller washcloth that I keep in my hipbelt pocket to mop at my brow, blow my nose, or whatever else I might need a clean(ish) cloth for.

No one talks about it on the trail, and most Camino narratives don't mention it, so I don't know if other people carry toilet paper with them. It certainly makes sense to unless you want to find a novel use for your extra pair of socks. You can buy travel-sized rolls at the drug store, but I find that travel packages of baby wipes are better. They hold up better, and you can use them to clean your hands and face as well (getting the order of these three uses right is crucial). As the classic *Everybody Poops* points out so well, they do this in Spain, too, so don't try to carry enough TP to last your whole trip. You can buy it in Europe, too. It's also smart to carry a small bottle of Purell or other hand sanitizer.

Regarding makeup, guidebooks and Camino narratives have a lot to say. I won't say much except that it's unnecessary. No pilgrim is looking their best. You might even say makeup stands out from the crowd in a negative way, plus you have to carry it. But if it makes you feel good, then go for it.

Washing your clothes

If you're going on just a week-long trip, you can purchase individual packets of laundry detergent in the travel section of local drug stores. Considering that you are only washing one outfit, the amount of soap in one of these packets is actually more soap than you need, but once opened, you can't reseal them, and besides, six or seven of these packets together weigh maybe an ounce and a half. Or a longer trip, plan on buying soap in villages. You can also use body soap or shampoo on your clothes.

There's no great secret to washing clothes by hand: fill a sink or tub with water and detergent, add in your clothes, make sure everything gets wet and soapy, and then...well, it was more clear to our great-grandmothers who had washboards and those roller bar thingies they would wring clothes in. If you're fortunate, the tub you're washing in has a kind of washboard attached to it and you can vigorously rub your clothes along it. Otherwise you just kind of rub your clothes vigorously against themselves to try to dislodge any dirt, and swirl them around in the water. Rinse until the water runs clear, or mostly clear anyway, wring them out as thoroughly as you can, and hang your clothes to dry on the clothesline. It leaves something to be desired relative to a modern washing machine, but as you look at your wash water, you'll see that you are indeed getting some nastiness out of your clothes.

You will need your own clothespins (at least one per item. I took one for each sock, one for my boxers, two for pants, and two for my shirt.) Many guidebooks recommend taking a length of cord of some sort for your own personal clothesline. I did once, but there was always a clothesline at the albergue. Even hotels along the Camino, at least the ones I've stayed in, had clotheslines. Worst case scenario, in my mind anyway, is that over the back of a chair, or even laying out flat on the grass on a sunny day, your clothes dry easily (because you bought the technical, quick-drying fabric!). Some albergues and hotels have washing machines (coin operated), and some will even do your laundry for a fee.

Medicine

I want to emphasize again that I am not a doctor, and I strongly recommend that you speak to your doctor about any medications you should take on the Camino, and I even more strongly urge you to follow your doctor's instructions and recommendations. What follows in the next several sections are what I take on my Camino and long hikes, and why. Always seek and follow your doctor's advice and instructions.

For prescription medications, take all you will need in the original bottles, and ask your doctor for a copy of the prescription with the generic name in case you need a refill while you're over in Europe. For the same reason, it's a good idea to have a list of all medical conditions you have, if any.

Pharmacies (*farmacias*) are easy to find in Spain. Ask the locals (*Donde esta la farmacia?*) and/or look for a white cross on a green background. Pharmacists in Spain are a little more hands on, especially on the Camino. They'll give you guidance on choosing a medication and treating blisters or other ailments.

One item you can ask your doctor about is the sleep-aid Ambien. I find it helps on the plane to knock me out for most of the flight, and it's helpful to combat jet lag, or a noisy albergue. Be warned that it is strong, can cause you to have vivid dreams, and some people have been known to behave strangely on it (including reports of Ambien users stripping nude on planes). Ask your doctor about it, and if he prescribes it for you, consider trying out a small dose at home before you leave to see how you react (following all the instructions from your doctor, of course). I took an Ambien about 45 minutes prior to my flight to Spain and within ten minutes found it difficult to stand and walk in a straight line – had my flight been delayed, I'd have had a serious problem. I've since learned to not take Ambien until I reach cruising altitude.

For over-the-counter medications, I take enough to last me ten days, and this is the only item I pack preparing for the worst. The reason I recommend this is because it's just easier if you know you're probably going to need some medications – you know what works for you.

First, Ibuprofen is such a hiking staple that it's picked up a nickname in hiking circles: Vitamin I. Hiking discomfort is about feet and joints and inflammation, so the anti-inflammatory properties of Vitamin I are much appreciated, as are the analgesic properties. I carry a small bottle.

Whether you're doing a bus tour or the Camino, perhaps diarrhea is the most common ailment among travelers. Personally, I suffer from Irritable Bowel Syndrome (IBS), so I'm very aware that strange dishes, high-fat food, stress, exhaustion, and bad luck can cause a case of diarrhea or make one worse. Whatever remedy you use at home, consider taking some with you on the Camino. You probably won't need to take as much with you as I take with me.

First aid kit

You need one in the hopes that you won't need one. I carry a small, one-person first aid kit supplemented with a few items.

What should a first aid kit contain? An assortment of Band-Aids and bandages in various sizes, tweezers, some cotton swabs, antibiotic ointment, burn ointment, a couple doses of OTC painkillers, and some safety pins. Any one-person first aid kit bought in an outdoor store should contain these and a few other items in a handy zippered pouch. I add a few more things to mine:

- Extra safety pins. They can fix a broken zipper and they can be used to hang still-wet socks or other items on your backpack to dry
- Small scissors
- Additional antibiotic ointment. If you get a blister, the small amount in the first aid kit may soon run out
- Earplugs. I found that they didn't help and actually kept me awake, but judging from Camino narratives, most people use these in the albergues to cut down on the snoring, talking, tossing, turning, and farting of their fellow pilgrims at night
- An emergency whistle. If you are injured, don't count on your cell phone working. Count on someone nearby hearing your very loud whistle (on the Camino, there's always someone nearby, or will be soon)
- Waterproof matches. I can't imagine an accident on the Camino that requires building a fire, but better to have them and not need them
- Extra batteries for my headlamp. This is a handy place to keep them
- Small, cheap flashlight. Just in case – there is no worse feeling than being stuck in the dark without any recourse
- Duct tape. You can wrap a few feet around a pencil or buy small rolls (about the size of your thumb) specifically for carrying on hikes. Whether to fix your gear or fix yourself, duct tape is a wonder tool

My first aid kit is also where I keep my blister treatment, and the top pocket of my pack is where I keep my first aid kit.

You might find in your practice hikes that your knees or ankles get especially sore. I can't count the number of time I've turned my ankles while hiking. I wear an elastic brace on both ankles. If you have any joint issues, speak with a knowledgeable healthcare professional about whether a device such as a brace will help you, and if so, take it with you on your Camino.

Electronics

I'm sure if you asked 10 veteran pilgrims whether you should take any electronics on the Camino, you'd get at least 11 opinions. Yes, I think it makes sense to carry some electronics on the Camino. I don't think they're distractions, I don't think they're barriers, and I don't think they should be used in lieu of talking to other pilgrims. I do think that you're halfway around the world, you have a lot of transit time, your life doesn't stop while you're gone, and electronics, especially smartphones, tablets, and cameras, are a valuable way to enhance your trip, add some convenience, and capture your experience. And I think this is especially true if you plan to do any traditional sightseeing in Europe, or in the major cities on the Camino.

The electronic you definitely need is a headlamp; no one disputes this. Spain is in the wrong time zone. Spain's 20th century dictator wanted Spain to be in the same time zone as the rest of Europe, so Spain is on Central European Time despite being further west than Britain, which is an hour behind Spain. The result is that it doesn't get light until late. You will be hiking in the dark first thing in the morning, and it will stay dark fairly late. Get yourself a good headlamp (not a flashlight) and carry an extra set of batteries. I keep my headlamp in the top pocket of my pack, but I take it out and leave it next to me on my bunk at night in case I need to get up and so I can see what I'm doing as I pack up in the morning.

I take my smart phone on the Camino and use it to connect to Wi-Fi occasionally. People back home will appreciate knowing you're okay and that they can get in touch with you, and you may appreciate being able to stay in touch. If you're traveling with a partner, a smartphone is especially convenient since most people hike at different paces.

Know your cell phone contract and the charges you could face for data, texts, and calls in Europe. If you are interested in being able to use your phone on European cell networks, you need to call your cell provider to unlock the phone and add international service. Depending on your device and provider, you may need to purchase a European SIM card (iPhones on the Sprint network don't have a SIM card, so you definitely need to buy one if you want to use your Sprint iPhone in Europe). A prepaid cell phone or SIM card in Europe is another option. I recommend seeking advice on this topic from your service provider and from a European travel guidebook for more information.

In addition to the need for a prepaid phone or SIM card in Europe, dialing is a little different. It's helpful to know two things. First, Spain's country code is 34. Second, some of Spain's area codes are three digits, and some are two.

- To call a Spanish number from the US, dial the international access code (011) then the country code (34) and then the area code and number.
- To call a Spanish number from within Spain, just dial the area code and number.
- To call a Spanish number from another European country, dial Europe's international access code (00), then the country code, then the area code and number.
- Finally, to call the US from within Europe, dial 00, then the US's country code (1) and then the area code and phone number.

Beyond just being a phone, though, I use my smartphone to make my travel easier. With the Internet access, I can use it to confirm reservations, book ahead, download information, store documents, and solve problems. It's my music player and my library on planes and trains, and you can even download audio guides for touring cities and sights. I don't recommend that anybody take a cell phone and plan on talking or texting or emailing with people daily – you want to be present on the Camino – but I also don't see a reason to not take advantage of the technology to enhance your experience and make travel easier. If you're worried about not being able to resist the temptation, just remember that it will cost a small fortune to call or text people while roaming in Europe. If you are taking your smartphone, disable data in the settings unless you plan to use, and pay for, data service. Be sure you understand your contract and what you'll be charged for while traveling – it adds up very quickly.

Some people take a tablet with them on the Camino such as an iPad or Kindle. I took my Kindle. I used it on the plane, but not on the Camino – I was too tired to read and more interested in my fellow pilgrims anyway. But a tablet is a good way to store important travel documents (see below).

Some guides suggest not taking a camera, feeling that they detract from being in the moment and build a wall of separation between you and the experience. I found that persuasive at first, but on my practice hikes I found myself occasionally taking out my phone to snap a picture. I ultimately decided that I did want to take a small point-and-shoot camera. As with everything, I searched for a camera that was small, light, and maximized functionality. I'm a not inexperienced photographer, so I'm well aware of the quality that gets lost with a point-and-shoot, but carrying several pounds of camera gear just isn't worth it. I chose a Canon Powershot SX260 for its size and for its zoom. I carry it in my pants pocket where I can get to it quickly. Remember to take extra batteries and memory cards (I take three of each).

If you're taking electronics, you'll have to take the chargers you need, and remember that you'll need a socket adaptor (European plugs are two *thin* round prongs, not to be confused with Korea's two *thick* round prongs). European electric grids are more powerful than American ones, so read your devices' manuals to be sure they can handle the extra power; if they can't, you'll need to buy a voltage adaptor (this is NOT the same as a socket adaptor). Most electronics work on both grids, but check yours just the same.

Take a watch. It's not necessary, but I found it handy, especially while in transit. You're probably used to using your smartphone, but bear in mind that you won't have it in your pocket all the time, and you'll need to be cognizant of saving the battery.

Miscellaneous

I find these things useful to have, for obvious reasons.

I carry a small pocketknife with a straight-edge blade. Maybe you'll need to cut a string, or a piece of cheese, or a blister pad – it's just handy to have. You can pick up a Swiss Army knife if you like, and that's probably a good idea if you plan on picnicking a lot. The corkscrew will be handy if you're a wine drinker.

D-rings, also called carabiners, are useful for hanging something off of your pack. I always carry one and just leave it hanging from a strap on my pack.

Bandanas are useful as just a piece of cloth. Get it wet and wrap it around your neck to stay cool, use it to clean your hands, or as a mini picnic mat.

I take a medium-sized but light nylon bag to use as travel bag on the plane ride over and on trains. I stuff it in the bottom of my pack while I'm on the Camino. At night, I place my phone, camera, wallet, and money belt in this bag and put it at the foot of my sleeping bag liner.

Should you take powerbars or other food? Perhaps a treat you really enjoy if it's small and lightweight, but food in Spain is plentiful and cheap. I'll own up to taking a few Clif bars with me, but only because I know they work well with my IBS in case my stomach is upset.

Items to help you organize

Some hikers don't like them, but I do: stuff sacks. The argument the folks who don't like stuff sacks make is that instead of a pack filled and full, you end up with a pack full of smaller bags, lumpy and difficult to distribute the weight. I think they exaggerate the former, I disagree about the latter, and I prioritize the convenience of having stuff sacks to organize my life on the Camino or any trail.

A stuff sack is just a nylon bag with a drawstring and a toggle to cinch it closed. They come in different sizes. Here's what I use:

- 1 medium sack to hold my second set of clothes
- 1 medium sack to hold my toiletries, including my towel (the extra room is helpful for taking your valuables with you to the shower)
- 1 small sack for holding my medications and electronic accessories
- 1 small sack for my underwear, socks, and sleeping shorts
- 1 small mesh sack for holding my laundry supplies

Compression sacks are stuff sacks with straps that can be tightened to squeeze out all the air and save space in your pack. If you're taking a sleeping bag, you definitely want one to make your sleeping bag easy to pack. In its compression sack, my 55-degree sleeping bag is about 6 inches long by 4 inches deep by 6 inches across, compared to a lot more volume when it's not compressed. I also use a compression sack to store my cold weather clothing. I figure these are the bulkiest item of clothing I'm carrying and the least likely I'll need.

The top pocket of your pack and the shovel pocket are sufficiently small that you don't need to worry about organizing those areas. Just focus on the main compartment, think about what will be in there, and how (and where) you're likely to use it.

A money belt is a pocket on an elastic strap that buckles around your waist under your clothes to foil pickpockets. Wear your money belt: keep your large bills, credit cards, passport, driver's license, insurance cards and travel tickets in your money belt, with smaller bills in your pocket or a wallet.

An alternative, which I like, is the hidden pocket. It's the pouch part of the money belt, but instead of an elastic strap, it has two belt loops. You thread your belt through it and then flip it over your waistband into your pants on your thigh. It's harder to access than a money belt, but I find it more comfortable when hiking.

Speaking of wallets, get a cheap nylon wallet for the Camino – your leather wallet will absorb sweat and get pretty funky. My wallet is where I keep that day's spending money (because even in Europe you get odd looks for reaching into your pants and coming up with a €20).

You can keep your other important documents in a Ziploc baggie in your travel bag.

Documents

I am not at all an expert on international travel, so this is absolutely an area where I recommend looking at a European travel guidebook for details. Here's what I take:

- A passport. But you do not need a visa in Western Europe
- Some other photo ID. Your driver's license is fine, and it's necessary if you will be renting a car in Europe. You need this in case you lose your passport
- Your health insurance card
- Your traveler's health insurance card. See below about travel insurance
- Your transportation tickets (the originals plus two copies)
- Your hotel reservations (the originals plus two copies)
- A list of contacts you might need and that somebody else might need. This should have your insurance information on it, phone numbers to contact your credit card companies, bank, and cell phone provider, the local embassy, your doctor, and your emergency contacts (with their title in the relevant language). This is also a good piece of paper to write down all your prescriptions and medical conditions.

You're probably printing out copies of your own tickets and reservations, so two copies should be sufficient. You can keep one copy in your money belt and one copy in your travel bag at the bottom of your pack. I use electronic boarding passes and documents while traveling in the US, but I prefer paper while abroad – don't count on the airports you are using to have that technology in place, or for it to be working if they do.

You will also need a photocopy of your passport and driver's license in case you lose either one. It's not a bad idea to memorize your passport number, driver's license number, and all your credit card information (including the pins) for just in case.

Do you need travelers' health insurance? It's cheap (mine was less than $20). Best case scenario you won't need any healthcare on your trip; worst case you do, and you're covered. Yes, Europe has a great socialized medical system, and yes, many doctors on the Camino will treat a pilgrim for free (according to rumor), but won't you feel better knowing that you're covered for the price of a modest dinner? Note, though, that most travelers' health insurance policies don't cover injuries sustained during certain activities, including hiking (or trekking, as they typically call it). You can get a special policy or supplement. Note also that your regular policy may cover certain kinds of care in Europe – read your policy.

Your smart devices are also useful for storing documents. Save an electronic copy on your smartphone and tablet if you have one AND email a copy to yourself. It will live in the cloud, accessible wherever there is Internet access. It's also a good idea to email a copy to your primary contact back home, along with your flight numbers and itinerary.

That's all you need. Easy, right? Just to help you out, I've included my packing list in the appendix.

What you don't need to take

Here are some things you don't need:

- A tent (unless you plan on sleeping outside)

- A sleeping pad (unless you plan on sleeping outside)
- A camping stove and fuel (no need to cook outdoors)
- A month's worth of anything, except prescription medications. You can buy what you need in Spain.
- "Nice" clothes or shoes. At least not on the trail. If you plan on doing some sightseeing that would include more than hiking apparel, you can mail it to yourself at the Santiago post office, your hotel, or the post office at where ever your destination is.

11. Conclusion

A pilgrimage is a mobile meditation, a chance to reflect on the course of our lives and our development as human beings. It matters little whether one embarks on pilgrimage for the adventure or for spiritual progress: there is no avoiding the changes that pilgrimage brings. Pilgrimage simplifies our lives, divests us of our belongings, breaks us down and builds us up again with new confidence. We are who we are on pilgrimage; all of our weaknesses and strengths are revealed and tested. And by going so far from our everyday lives, we temporarily shed the many roles that we play, the roles we use to protect ourselves from the world, the roles that keep us from having to be honest with ourselves and each other. Far from being escapist, pilgrimage is where we are most real.

When you return, you'll find that you remember every detail of your journey. You'll think about your Camino almost daily. You will test the patience of your friends and family as you talk and talk about the Camino. But the hardest part of the return is holding on to the lessons you learned, the breakthroughs you made, the person you discovered yourself to be.

This world will try to force you to be the person that is most useful to everyone but yourself. While you lived happily out of a backpack for a month, you will struggle with the materialistic impulses and minor dramas that occupy our days but don't fill up our souls. The stress of our disconnected modern world will gradually chip away at the sense of serenity that pilgrimage fosters. I've given you much information on how to physically prepare for the Camino, but only you can mentally and spiritually prepare yourself for the rigors of pilgrimage and for the return to the world we've constructed for ourselves.

My brief time on the Camino was the happiest of my adult life. For a few days, I understood what it means to be truly free – to be able to go anywhere my feet could carry me, to live by my own sense of time, to do or not do as I chose. And like every pilgrim, upon returning I have struggled to live my life as the person I was on the Camino. From what I have observed, there is only one way to hold on to that better self: to go on pilgrimage again.

I hope you experience the same joy and find whatever it is you seek on the way to Santiago.

Buen Camino.

January 2017

Part IV

Appendix

11. My Camino packing list

Items on my person
- Backpack
- Sunglasses
- Hiking boots
- Hiking outfit (hiking socks, underwear, pants/shorts, t-shirt)
- Trekking poles
- Baseball cap
- Wristwatch

Top pocket of my pack
- **Loose**
  - Headlamp
  - Baby wipes
  - Boot laces
  - Bandana
  - Sunscreen
  - Sunglasses case
  - Hand Sanitizer
  - Headphones (in small case)

- **First aid kit**
  - **In addition to the kit...**
    - Duct tape
    - Extra batteries for your head lamp
    - Emergency whistle
    - Molefoam

- **Laundry sack**
  - Clothes pins (7 of them)
  - Laundry soap packets

Main Compartment
- **Food sack (at the top of the compartment)**
  - Clif bars
  - Picnic lunch or snack
- **Toiletries sack**
  - Shower towel
  - Ear plugs
  - Shampoo
  - Toothpaste
  - Tooth brush
  - Comb
  - Soap
  - Deodorant
  - Prescription medications
  - Ibuprofen
  - Imodium
  - Ambien

- **Electronics sack (next to food sack at the top of the compartment)**
  - Plug adapter
  - Smartphone
  - Phone charger
  - Camera (in small case)
  - Camera charger
  - Memory cards
  - Camera batteries

- **Clothing sack (middle of main compartment)**
  - Hiking pants
  - Hiking shirt
  - Button front shirt
  - Gym shorts
  - Hiking socks
  - Boxer-briefs

- **Cold weather sack (next to clothing sack in the middle of the compartment)**
  - Long underwear
  - Fleece hat

- Gloves
  - Fleece jacket

- **Sleeping bag liner (in it's own compression sack, down at the very bottom of the main compartment)**

- **Sandals (stuffed on either side at the bottom of the pack**

- **Travel day bag (for plane and train rides)**
  - Kindle

Hipbelt pockets
- Washcloth
- Pocket knife

Shovel pocket
- Rain cover
- Rain jacket
- D-ring (clipped to the outside)

Side pockets
- Credencial
- Nalgene bottle

Hydration sleeve
- 2-Liter hydration bladder

Money belt
- Cash
- Passport
- Health insurance card
- Travel health insurance card
- Train tickets
- Hotel reservations (if any)
- Plane tickets
- List of contacts, medications, and medical conditions
- Debit card
- Credit card

Pants pockets
- Wallet
- Camera
- Camino guidebook pages

12. A few Spanish words and phrases

Type	English	Spanish
Greeting	Hello	Hola
	Good morning	Buenos días
	Good afternoon	Buenas tardes
	Good evening	Buenas noches
	Goodnight	Buenas Noches
	Goodbye	Adiós
	My name is...	Mi nombre es.../ Me llamo es...
Language	Do you speak English?	Habla usted Inglés?
	I do not speak Spanish	Yo no hablo español
	Can you please repeat that?	¿Puedes por favor repetir eso?
	I'm sorry, I don't understand	Lo siento, no entiendo
Polite	Thank you	Gracias/ Graciñas (Galicia only)
	Please	Por Favor
	Sir	Señor
	Madaam	Señora
	Excuse me	Discúlpeme
	I'm sorry	Lo siento
	How are you?	Cómo estás?
	I am good	Estoy bien.
	I am bad	Soy malo.
People	Man	Hombre
	Woman	Mujer
	Boy/Girl	Niño/Niña

Type	English	Spanish
Tourist	Is this the entrance?	¿Es esta la entrada?
	Where is the exit?	Donde esta la salida?
	Where is the toilet/ bathroom/restroom?	Donde esta el baño/ baño/aseos?
Conversation	Yes	Sí
	No	No
	I don't know	No lo sé
Shopping and Eating	May I have the bill now?	¿Puedo tener la cuenta ahora?
	How much does it cost?	Cuánto cuesta?
	Chicken	Pollo
	Pasta	Pasta
	Potato	Patatas
	French fries	Papas fritas
	Apple	Manzana
	I would like an apple, please	Quiero un manzana, por favor
Sleeping	A room	Una habitación
	A bed	Una cama
	Shower	Ducha
	I have a reservation	Tengo una reserva
	My phone number is...	Mi número de teléfono es ...
	May I leave my bag at the desk?	¿Puedo dejar mi bolsa en el escritorio?
Weather	What is the weather tomorrow?	¿Cuál es el tiempo mañana?
	Sunny	Soleado
	Rain	Lluvia
	Hot	Caliente
	Cold	Frío
	Pleasant	Agradable

Type	English	Spanish
Directions	Where is...	Dónde está ...
	Right	Derecha
	Left	Izquierda
	Straight	Derecho
	Backward	Hacia atrás
	North	Norte
	South	Sur
	East	Oriente
	West	Oeste
Time	What time?	Qué hora?
	What time is it?	Qué hora es?
	It is 14:00 o'clock.	Es 14:00 en punto.
	Today	Hoy
	Tomorrow	Mañana
	Yesterday	Ayer
Numbers	Zero	Cero
	One	Uno
	Two	Dos
	Three	Tres
	Four	Cuatro
	Five	Cinco
	Six	Seis
	Seven	Siete
	Eight	Ocho
	Nine	Nueve
	Ten	Diez
	Hundred	Cien
	Thousand	Mil

Type	English	Spanish
Camino	Pilgrim	Peregrino/Peregrina
	Bicycle pilgrim	Bicigrino/Bicigrina
	I am walking the Camino de Santiago	Estoy caminando el Camino de Santiago
	Yellow arrow	Flecha amarillas
	How far is it to the next village?	Qué distancia hay a la siguiente pueblo?
	Common Camino greeting and farewell	Buen Camino!
Travel	Airport	Aeropuerto
	Bus	Autobus
	Train	Tren
	Bus/Train station	Estacion de autobuses/trenes
	Ticket	Billete
	Bus stop	Parada de autobuses
	Taxi	Taxi

13. Good resources for learning more about the Camino

American Pilgrims on the Camino. You can get your credencial here, and their website includes a wealth of information.

Caminodesantiago.me, an English-language forum on the Camino, mostly visited by Americans. You can get the latest information about the Camino and get more of your questions answered here.

Rick Steves' website. His company, Europe Through The Backdoor, is probably the best resource of information about traveling to Europe.

And lastly, a few authors whose Camino books were arguably responsible for the rebirth of the Camino: Hape Kerkeling, Shirley MacClaine, Paul Coelho.

Finally, please leave a review of this book on Amazon. I look to these reviews to improve the information I make available to pilgrims, and if you found this book helpful, you can help your fellow pilgrims by letting them know as well. Buen Camino!

About the Author

Ryan is a statistician by trade, a hiker by choice, and a pilgrim by calling. He resides in St. Louis and hits the trail whenever he can. This is his first book.

Made in the USA
San Bernardino, CA
14 January 2018